The Gift of Christmas Past

The Gift of
Christmas Past
A Return to Victorian Traditions

Text by Sunny O'Neil
Drawings by Dennis O'Neil

The American Association for State and Local History
Nashville, Tennessee

Author and publisher make grateful acknowledgment for permission to use in this book material from the following sources:

America's Christmas Heritage, by Ruth Cole Kainen. Published by Funk and Wagnall's. Copyright © 1969 by Ruth Cole Kainen. Excerpts on pages 96, 104, 113–114, and 123–124 reprinted by permission of Harper and Row, Publishers, Inc.

The American Heritage Cookbook. Copyright © 1964 by the American Heritage Publishing Company, Inc. Excerpts on pages 114–115, 125–126, and 126–127 reprinted by permission from the American Heritage Publishing Company, Inc.

The Boston Cooking School Cookbook, by Fannie Merritt Farmer, published by Little, Brown and Company, 1947. Excerpt on page 112 reprinted by permission of the Fanny Farmer Cookbook Corporation.

Christmas Decorations from Williamsburg's Folk Art Collection, published by the Colonial Williamsburg Foundation, 1976; distributed by Holt, Rinehart and Winston. Excerpts on pages 47 and 55 reprinted by permission from Beatrix T. Rumford, Director and Vice-President of Museums, the Abby Aldrich Rockefeller Folk Art Center.

Cookie Cookery, by John Zenker and Hazel G. Zenker. Copyright © 1969 by Hazel G. Zenker. Excerpts on pages 118–119 reprinted by permission of the publisher, M. Evans and Company, Inc., New York.

The Holiday Candy Book, by Virginia Pasley. Copyright © 1952 by Virginia Pasley. Excerpt on page 15 reprinted by permission of Little, Brown and Company, in association with the Atlantic Monthly Press.

Mark Twain Memorial, Hartford, Connecticut. Excerpt on page 120 reprinted by permission of Wynn Lee, Director.

Maryland's Way, by Mrs. Lewis R. Andrews and Mrs. J. Reancy Kelly, published in 1963 by the Hammond-Harwood House Association. Excerpt on page 115 reprinted by permission of the Hammond-Harwood House Association.

Library of Congress Cataloguing-in-Publication Data
O'Neil, Sunny.
      The gift of Christmas past.
      Bibliography: p.
      1. Christmas—United States—History. 2. Christmas decorations—United States—History.
3. Christmas cookery. 4. Christmas decorations—United States.
I. Title.
GT4986.A1053   394.2′68282   81-14961
ISBN 0-910050-55-4   AACR2

Second Printing 1982

Publication of this book was made possible in part by funds from the sale of the Bicentennial State Histories, which were supported by the National Endowment for the Humanities.

Designed by John Halliburton

This book is dedicated
to my loving husband Ralph
and to the rest of my wonderful family

Contents

Illustrations

Acknowledgments

My grateful thanks to these people for their help! All of the librarians at Little Falls Library, Montgomery County, Maryland; Margot Bronner of the Morris Library at the University of Delaware; the staff at the Stowe-Day Foundation, with a special thanks to Ellice Schofield; to Wynn Lee at the Mark Twain Memorial; to Peter Van Wingen, Rare Books and Special Collections, the Library of Congress; to Mr. Fargus at the National Agricultural Library, Educational Research Division; and to Perry Fisher of the Columbia Historical Society.

More thanks to: Rhoda Baer, Linda Bartlett, James R. Buckler, Joan Burka, Barbara Freeman, Myron Hayslett, Andy Leon Harney, John Monday, Lauranne C. Nash, Lois Over, Rodris Roth, William Seale, Dortha H. Skelton, Enola Teeter, Alan Zins, and Eleanor Zins.

My undying gratitude goes to Phillip V. Snyder, a real Christmas person, and author of *The Christmas Tree Book*.

Preface: Recreating the American Victorian Christmas

This book is for everyone who loves the Victorian Christmas and would like to reproduce it as closely and authentically as possible. Up to now, restorationists, decorators, staffs and volunteers at museums and historic houses built in the 1800s have found only meager guidelines to help in developing Christmas ornaments and decorations authentic to the Victorian period. For them, for private owners of historic houses, and for all others who would like to recreate an authentic Victorian atmosphere at Christmas, we have put this book together, showing how to make Christmas tree ornaments, table settings, and room decorations in an authentic manner reflecting the period between 1837 and 1901, using today's materials.

Once the decorations establishing the Victorian Christmas atmosphere are in place, the planning of Victorian dinners and parties to round out the season is a natural sequence; and for those festivities, recipes and games are included.

We hope that all who cherish Victorian houses will find these gleanings a source of inspiration in decorating the house, adapting the ideas presented here to the size of the house, the pocketbook, and the energies of those responsible for it.

The religious significance of Christmas has not been touched on in this book, but it was at the heart of the true Victorian's Christmas celebration; indeed, the religious spirit carried Victorians through the season with reminders that no one should be forgotten: it was a time for caring about the sick, the poor, and the lonely.

While searching out information on ways to bring about a truly Victorian Christmas today, our feeling of nostalgia was fired by the Victorians' own plaint of Christmases gone by and a yearning for "the good old days."

Children's excitement on the "Night before Christmas" endures, as in this timeless etching.

I Gifts

This chapter on gifts is included in a book primarily about Victorian decorations because gifts were often used as ornaments on the Christmas tree and were also placed under the tree.

For the Victorians, preparations for Christmas-gift exchanges started weeks in advance of the big day. Although many presents were made at home, the shops were filled with all sorts of goods in abundance.

There was great concern about the holiday becoming too commercial and a "festival of store-keepers," as one editor put it, in a current issue of *The Ladies' Home Journal*.[1] That theme was repeated in many publications of the time; but considering the profusion of objects for sale overflowing the shelves, no one paid much attention to the admonition.

For those far way from the big city stores, plenty of things could be ordered through the mail; advertisements for toys, silver, and trinkets of all kinds were found in magazines and newspapers.

Another good Victorian source for presents was the charity bazaar. The making of Christmas gifts was started far ahead of the season, not only to finish creating things for family and friends in plenty of time, but also to have ready items to be donated to these "Fancy Fairs."[2]

Making Christmas presents served a twofold purpose in the life of a Victorian woman: it helped to make money for a worthy cause, and it was a genuine form of recreation. Needlework, since it was so time-consuming, was worked on constantly; but in between needlework projects, other objects were put together.

Gifts of food were also popular—preserves, conserves, jams, and jellies that had been made in the summer, and candy, which could be made any time.[3]

The periodicals of the day gave pages of advice to their readers on how to shop, what to shop for, and how to distribute the fruits of their labors.

Period descriptions of the stores and the crowds varied with the age and circumstance of the observer. In a December 1892 issue of the *Ladies' Home Journal*, a practical, middle-aged writer advises her readers to begin their Christmas shopping early in December, when goods were fresh, shops free of crowds, and the salespeople unfatigued. Another writer suggests giving money, especially to young married couples just starting out in life.

A younger point of view appears in the December 1852 issue of *Peterson's*

Magazine. There, the heroine of a story writes home to her mother in the country of the thrill of being in the city on Christmas Eve afternoon. As she walked along looking into the shop windows, she wrote, she felt as if she had been transported back into *The Arabian Nights*, she was so dazzled by the array of toys, work boxes, books, and jewelry gleaming brightly in store after store. She told of fathers hurrying home with baskets full of turkeys, cranberries, celery, and apples, and mothers carrying dolls and toys of all kinds home for the children. She describes laughing schoolgirls, carrying muffs filled with small toys and candies for younger brothers and sisters, their faces aglow with the pleasure of anticipated giving, and leaves the reader envisioning the Victorian Christmas as a carnival of mirth and happiness for children, parents, and even playful dogs.

Presents of plants were welcomed by the Victorians—no group loved flowers more than they. They also enjoyed "uplifting" tales and never missed an opportunity to moralize. An example is the high-minded story of a poor family given a sturdy, blooming red geranium. This bright spot in their lives inspired family members to wash their windows, to give the plant sunshine; then, because the newly cleaned windows were such a contrast to the rest of the house, they scrubbed floors and cleared out corners, and soon the careless, untidy family became neat, painstaking, and prosperous! And to think that this all happened because of choosing the right present for the right people!

Writers of the day made suggested gift lists for everyone. Presents such as doilies, silver tea balls, and tea strainers for the hostess' table were popular; and for the parlor, there were photograph frames in silver, fabric, or leather. For the bedroom, dressing-table mirrors were suggested, and boxes, fans, vases, and jewelry were said to be welcome additions.[4]

Gifts for men included cigars and cigarette cases, scarves and mufflers. Advice on jewelry for men held that, to be appropriate, such personal items should be rare or grotesque, rather than fine and pretty. Writers also suggested adding an umbrella to the list, because men seemed to have an unlimited capacity for umbrellas. A good whip or a carriage robe was also recommended.

For grandmothers who enjoyed knitting, a "wonder ball" headed the list. A "wonder ball" was a ball of yarn carefully unraveled and rewound with many little gifts hidden inside. The gifts were revealed as the yarn was

As social commentary, "The Morning after Christmas" reveals Victorian children as marvelously decorous.

gradually used up in knitting. Add to the "wonder ball" a footstool, a pot of primroses, a folding fruit knife, and a screen against draughts, and the Victorian grandmother would indeed have a merry Christmas, the columnists wrote.

Boys of Victorian times were said to enjoy receiving tool boxes, boxing gloves, sleds and skates, stamps and stamp albums, lanterns, jackknives, books of adventure, cap pistols, and marbles.

Little girls, it was said, rejoiced in gifts that imitated those of older sisters: a party fan, a bit of jewelry, a sachet, note paper with a monogram, books, perhaps a canary—for a girl fond of pets—and always a doll or two, depending on her age.

Everyone expected and usually got an orange in the toe of the Christmas stocking; but in the American South, boys and girls alike looked forward to a package of Chinese firecrackers, which they exploded all day long. Christmas time down South meant noise and plenty of it.[5]

Clothes were always included as presents for young and old alike, and much time was spent knitting mittens, mufflers, and socks, as well as stitching up aprons, waistcoats, and the like.

When it came to distributing gifts, everyone was remembered. A good example of Victorian largesse was Mrs. Samuel L. Clemens, wife of Mark Twain. Mrs. Clemens turned their guest room into Santa's workshop. There presents were wrapped, and many baskets were filled for the sick and the needy. In addition to preparing gifts for all her family, far and near, and her neighbors, Mrs. Clemens remembered her servants and their families. Her gift list included fruit, candy, paintings, books, coin banks, beads, combs, ice skates, and handkerchiefs. Her daughters helped her, and they started months ahead of the holiday.[6]

Since organized charities outside the church were rare, most middle-class women assembled gifts for boxes for the poor, along with their own families' presents.

Near Leesburg, Virginia, Oatlands Mansion, a property of the National Trust for Historic Preservation open to the public, is decorated for Christmas in November. The staff at Oatlands used the following letter, written by the granddaughter of the original owners, as a source of information for their Victorian Christmas open house:

> Our thoughts are turned to Christmas and we had many happy hours planning and making out our long Christmas list. The two dollars Father gave to each of us seemed a fortune and it meant a day in Leesburg and a visit to Mr. Beeler's store. We bought sachet, ribbons, embroidery thread, lots of drawing paper and even more blotting paper as Curtis was a great painter of book marks and calenders and we made these by the dozens. We mostly depended on Mother's Rag Bag and here we got our inspiration for our best presents. We made sachets, needle cases, pen wipers, and pomander balls.[7]

Many gifts, such as those mentioned in the letter, were hung on the tree. The following gift ideas are included here because they serve a dual purpose: they would make charming and unusual gifts today, and they also lend themselves to use as ornaments for a Victorian Christmas tree. Perhaps fashioning items such as these in the atmosphere of yesterday may also prove a relaxing form of recreation today.

4

Wooden-Spoon Pincushion

Materials needed:
Wooden spoon with long
   handle
Paint
Pincushion
Glue
Ribbon

Tools needed:
Paintbrush
Scissors

Hanging pincushions were thought to be exceedingly convenient, and wooden spoons were used to make them. Paint or gild the wooden spoon and fill its bowl with a pincushion securely glued in place. Decorate the spoon handle near the top with a pretty ribbon bow, with ends from which to suspend the spoon.

SOURCE: *American Agriculturist*, December 1889, p. 640.

A Dainty Watch Case

Materials needed:
Lightweight cardboard
Red silk fabric
White satin fabric
Chamois (optional)
Ribbon
Small fabric ornament
Glue
Thread
Tools needed:
Scissors
Needle
Felt-tipped pen with fine
   point
Liquid embroidery pen (optional)

Cut four round pieces of cardboard 3¼ inches in diameter. Cover two of them with red silk, and the other two with white satin, or chamois skin, for the lining. Take a strip of the red silk 12½ inches long and 3 inches wide and make a narrow hem on the two ends. Gather the two sides and stitch them onto the wrong side of each white round, just inside the edge, leaving 3¼ inches for the opening.

Take one yard of half-inch ribbon and cut it in two pieces of equal length. Sew one end of each piece on the wrong side of the white rounds and tie the two ends in a bow to hang the watch case up by.

Stick a small ornament (embroidered design decal) in the center of one of the red rounds, with the words "You sleep, I'll watch" painted or written in gilt or black above it. Paste the red rounds to the white ones.

SOURCE: *The Ladies' Home Journal*, December 1890, p. 17.

Chamois Eyeglass Cleaner

Materials needed:

Paper for pattern
Chamois
Narrow lavender ribbon
Ink
Thread

Tools needed:

Scissors
Pen
Needle
Felt-tipped pen with fine point
Pencil

Cut a piece of paper in the form of a heart, and from this pattern make two hearts of soft, smooth chamois. Bind each with narrow lavender ribbon. On one heart, draw a pair of eyeglasses in outline with a fine pen and ink (or a felt-tipped pen with a fine point), after sketching them in pencil.

Using the buttonhole stitch, sew the hearts together, forming a bag, with the opening at the top of the hearts. Finish by ornamenting the point of the heart, at the bottom, with a bow of the narrow lavender ribbon.

The chamois is excellent for rubbing the glasses free of all dust.

SOURCE: *The Ladies' Home Journal*, November 1890, p. 9.

Bags of All Kinds

Workbag

Materials needed:

Fabric: silk, satin, or velvet
Box
Glue
Cord
Thread

Tools needed:

Scissors
Needle

A workbag can be made by covering a box (without a lid) with silk, satin, or velvet. The box should be twelve inches long and three inches wide, with sides three inches high. (These measurements are approximate.) A bag of satin or silk to match the box is fitted inside and finished off with a casing at the top to hold the indispensable cord to act as closure and hanger.

Marble Bags

Materials needed: *Tools needed:*
Bright scrap fabrics   Scissors
Thread   Needle
String or cord

Small boys always welcomed marble bags. Marble bags can be made of odd pieces of sturdy cotton fabric about five inches long and three inches wide, stitched on three sides (two long and one short), right sides together. Before turning the bag right-side out, make a casing for the cord or string.

Source: *American Agriculturist*, December 1889, p. 640.

A Slipper Bag

Materials needed: *Tools needed:*
Stiff cardboard   Scissors
Bright cotton   Needle
Elastic
Brass ring
Thread

To make a slipper bag that hangs on the wall, you will need a piece of stiff cardboard 15 inches long, 4 inches wide at the bottom, and 6 inches across the top, which should be sloped to a blunt point. Cover both sides of the cardboard form neatly with bright cotton fabric. Take another piece of the matching fabric 13 inches long, 10½ inches wide at the bottom, and 15 inches at the top. Make a hem 1 inch wide at the top. Below the hem, gather twice and run a piece of elastic through. Fold two box pleats at the bottom, and sew it to the back piece, leaving the top open to admit the slippers. This opening should not be so wide that the hem falls over, but just wide enough for the slippers to enter. The top of the hem in the middle should be 5 inches from the top of the point.

Sew a brass ring on the point, and the bag is finished; and according to the November 1884 issue of *Harper's Young People* magazine, "A very pretty and useful article you will find it."

Source: *Harper's Young People*, November 1884, p. 14.

A Novel Workbag

Materials needed:
Straw hat
Dye or varnish (optional)
Silk fabric
Thread
Sobo glue
Narrow ribbon

Tools needed:
Scissors
Needle
Paintbrush

A novel workbag can be made of the crown of a straw hat, which may be dyed or varnished, painted, or left in its natural color. Coat the inside of the treated hat with glue; then line it with silk of a harmonizing color, continuing the silk beyond the straw crown sufficiently to form a bag.

Finish with a hem as a casing wide enough to admit a double runner of narrow ribbon with which to draw up the mouth of the bag.

SOURCE: *American Agriculturist*, December 1889, p. 640.

A Checkerboard Scent Bag

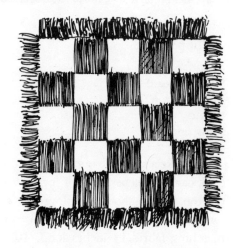

Materials needed:
Scarlet ribbon
Pale blue ribbon
Thread
Cotton (or polyester fiber) for
    stuffing
Heliotrope sachet
    powder (see "Sources")

Tools needed:
Scissors
Needle

A young Victorian lady explains to a friend, in an 1884 issue of *Harper's Young People*, just how she went about making her Christmas gifts:

"To make this scent bag I bought a piece of scarlet ribbon sixty inches long, and as much more of pale blue, each three-quarters of an inch wide, and cut each ribbon in ten pieces. Then I placed five of the red strips side by side, and wove the blue ones in and out checkerboard fashion. I did the same with the other ribbons, and fringed out the ends.

"After stitching three sides together I put some heliotrope powder on a bit of cotton and placed it inside the bag then stitched the fourth side."

SOURCE: *Harper's Young People,* 18 November 1884, p. 44.

A Wastebasket

Materials needed:
Paper parasol
Fine wire
Wooden block
Glue
Ribbon

Tools needed:
Darning needle
Heavy scissors or wire cutters
Drill

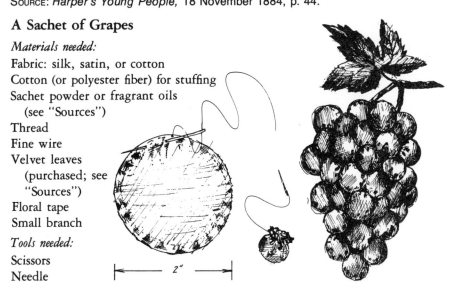

Our young lady of the scent bag
continues explaining her list of gifts with
directions for making a wastebasket:

"A wastebasket is easily made from a Japanese paper umbrella. Make
holes in the wooden spoke ends with a darning needle. Open the umbrella
(or parasol) half-way and put fine wire through the holes, twist the ends
together, and in this way the parasol will remain in its half-open state.

"Insert the parasol into a hole which has been drilled in a block of wood,
and glue in place so that it will remain stationary.

"A ribbon bow in the proper color is attached to the handle giving a
finishing touch to this lovely addition to a room."
SOURCE: *Harper's Young People,* 18 November 1884, p. 44.

A Sachet of Grapes

Materials needed:
Fabric: silk, satin, or cotton
Cotton (or polyester fiber) for stuffing
Sachet powder or fragrant oils
    (see "Sources")
Thread
Fine wire
Velvet leaves
    (purchased; see
    "Sources")
Floral tape
Small branch

Tools needed:
Scissors
Needle

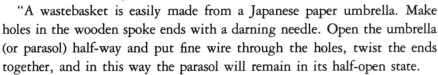

|← 2″ →|

9

Sachets were very well received in Victorian homes and were made in many forms and fragrances. This one, made to look like a bunch of grapes, is novel and practical in that it is a good way to use up sewing scraps. It is ideal to hang on the tree, too, since it is quite decorative.

Silk, satin, or cotton in any grape color may be used.

Follow sketches on page 9: cut each grape from a piece of fabric two inches square. Work small stitches near the outer edge, fill the center with scented cotton, and pull the thread, tying or stitching it securely. Fine wire should be wrapped over the pulled thread to serve as a stem. Leave the wire stems two or three inches long, so that individual grapes may be taped together to form a cluster. Tape to a small branch and add a velvet leaf.

SOURCE: *Needle and Brush*, Metropolitan Art Series (New York: The Butterick Publishing Co., Lt., 1889), p. 66.

A Banana Sachet

Materials needed:
Banana
Paper
Yellow ribbon
Yellow cotton fabric
Cotton (or polyester fiber)
    for stuffing
Sachet powder
    or fragrant oils
    (see "Sources")
Thread

Tools needed:
Scissors
Pencil
Needle
Paintbrush
Brown felt-tipped pen

Another fruit-inspired sachet is made in the form of a banana. Take a well-shaped banana and peel it carefully, separating the peeling at the "seams." Lay each piece of peel on a piece of paper and mark with a pencil the exact shape and size; cut out the paper, not allowing for seams. (If that seems too much trouble, use graph paper to enlarge the drawings above.)

As you draw the paper pattern, number the pieces as you mark, so that you will be sure to get them in the proper order when you put them together; some of the pieces will be so nearly alike that it will be difficult to determine their exact place, otherwise, and one piece out of place will spoil the whole shape.

Take canary-colored fabric (material with a little "give" is best). The amount needed will depend on the number of sachets you wish to make, but a piece of fabric approximately fifteen inches square should be enough for one. Using the paper pattern you have cut or traced from "life" or from your graph-paper drawing, outline in pencil on the fabric and cut out the pieces, leaving about a quarter of an inch for the seam.

The pencil marks will be a guide for sewing. Leave a small opening at the large end and carefully fill with soft cotton, scented with fragrance.

SOURCE: *The Ladies' Home Journal*, July 1890, p. 23.

Wheat Sachet

Materials needed:

Approximately 25 stalks of wheat
String
Cotton
    (or polyester fiber)
    for stuffing
Narrow baby ribbon
Fragrant oil
Powdered sachet   }   (See "Sources")

Tools needed:

Scissors
Safety pin

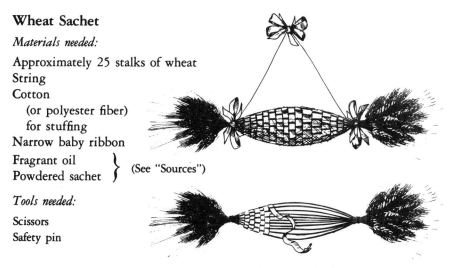

A sachet of wheat, according to an early issue of the *American Agriculturist*, makes a pretty ornament, as well as a welcome gift.

To make a wheat-stalk sachet, take about twenty-five stalks of wheat, each eight inches long, and tie them around a wad of cotton that has been scented with oils or powder at each end. If the wheat is dry, soak it in water first, to make it more pliable.

Let the soaked stalks dry; then attach a safety pin to the end of narrow baby ribbon and weave the ribbon in and out through the straws and tie up with bows at the ends. Cut off the frayed ends and the pin. Tie more ribbon to be used as a hanger with a bow on top, as seen in the drawing.

SOURCE: *American Agriculturist*, July 1890, p. 408.

Pomander Ball

Materials needed:

Apple
Whole cloves
Cinnamon (ground)
Orris root (optional—
   see "Sources")
Ribbon
Bird or other trim

Tools needed:

Adhesive tape
Paper bag
Scissors

Pomander balls are decorative, as well as fragrant; they may be placed in a closet, piled in a bowl, or, during the Christmas season, hung on the Christmas tree.

A pomander ball is easily made from an apple and whole cloves. Wrap your thumb in both directions—around and up and down—with adhesive tape and push the whole cloves into the apple with the protected thumb. When the apple is completely covered (cover it all in one sitting; if left half-finished even overnight, it will spoil), place it in a paper bag with ground cinnamon and orris root and shake it. When the apple is well powdered, put it in a warm, dry place. If you put it in the kitchen, you will enjoy the fragrance as it dries. Turn it from time to time, so it won't develop any flat spots. The pomander should be dry in about two weeks. As the apple dries, it shrinks, so wait until it is thoroughly dry before wrapping with ribbon and trim.

SOURCE: Brochure, "Oatlands" (Washington, D.C.: National Trust for Historic Preservation, n.d.).

Lace-Glove Potpourri

Materials needed:

Paper for pattern
Lace
Cotton fabric
Cotton or polyester fiber for stuffing
Fragrant oils or powdered sachet
Ribbon
Thread

Tools needed:

Pencil
Scissors
Needle

Use your hand as a guide and trace around it on a piece of paper. Cut out the paper "hand" pattern, allowing a half-inch for the seam. Cut one piece of lace and another of plain cotton. Stitch the pieces together on the wrong side. Cut deeply into the fabric between the fingers, so that when it is turned to the right side, each finger will be clearly defined.

Stuff the glove with cotton (or polyester fiber) perfumed with fragrant oil or powdered sachet. Tie a ribbon into a bow around the wrist and add a lace frill. (See color section, Plate 6.)

SOURCE: Author's collection.

Dainty Christmas Candy Boxes

Materials needed:

Colored cardboard
(posterboard)
Glue
(Elmer's, Sobo, etc.)
Acrylic paint
(optional)
Colored papers
(optional)
Ribbon bows

Tools needed:

Scissors
Dull knife
Spring-type clothespins
Pencil

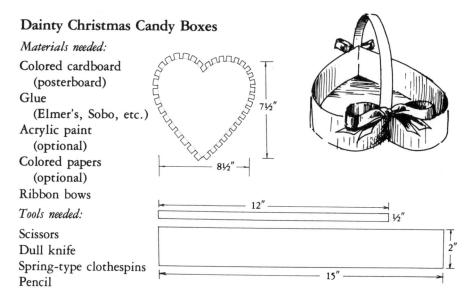

To make the heart-shaped box shown in the drawing, cut the base out of light-weight strips of cardboard. Cut two long, straight strips of the cardboard, each equal in width to the desired depth of the box, long enough to fit around the heart shape and to provide for a lap to join the ends of the strip together. Fold up the flaps around the base; paste one strip of cardboard on the outside and the other on the inside.

Cut two strips a half-inch wide and twelve inches long for the handle. Glue the strips together for strength, then glue to the outside of the box (the clothespins come in handy for holding the handle in place, as the glue dries). Cover the ends with bows of ribbon.

Many publications carried designs for boxes, but I felt that these two, in an 1897 *Ladies' Home Journal*, were the most unusual.

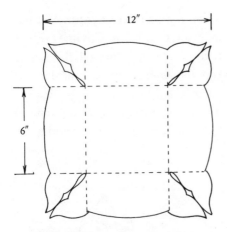

The butterfly box is made of a similar light-weight cardboard. Draw the outline as shown in the drawing; cut out, and run a dull knife along the lines to be folded. Then glue the corners together on the fold, as shown. The butterflies that are formed by gluing these corners may be painted, or another piece of colored paper can be overlaid on the cardboard in a colorful butterfly design.

Cut two strips a half-inch wide and twelve inches long for the handle; glue them together for strength; then glue them to the inside of the box. Line the box with tissue paper and fill with candy or small gifts.

Bonbons of all kinds were popular in the 1800s, either purchased or made at home. When homemade candy was placed in lovely, handmade boxes, it was doubly appreciated.

SOURCE: *The Ladies' Home Journal*, December 1897, p. 10.

The recipes that follow have been brought up to date, as far as measurements and ingredients are concerned, while still being kept as accurate and authentic to the period as possible.

Peanut Brittle

3 cups white sugar	3 cups warm raw Spanish peanuts
1 cup hot water	⅓ stick of butter
1½ cups light Karo syrup	1 teaspoon vanilla
1 teaspoon salt	1 heaping teaspoon baking soda

Put all ingredients except peanuts and butter in a heavy four-quart pan.

Use a candy thermometer and heat to 240 degrees. Add nuts and butter; cook, stirring constantly with a wooden spoon, to 300 degrees.

Remove from the heat immediately. Stir in vanilla and baking soda. Pour onto buttered marble slab (a buttered cookie sheet is a good substitute) and pull with buttered fingers until the candy is very thin. This step is very important and makes the candy absolutely melt in the mouth.

Wrap in waxed paper or colorful tissue paper, fringing the ends.

SOURCE: *The Ladies' Home Journal*, January 1890, p. 19.

Chocolate Fudge

2 cups sugar	3 tablespoons cocoa
⅓ cup corn syrup	3 tablespoons butter
⅔ cup milk	1 teaspoon vanilla

Place all the ingredients except butter and vanilla over low heat and stir carefully until ingredients are well-mixed and the sugar is dissolved. Continue stirring until mixture begins to boil; then put in the candy thermometer and cook over medium heat, stirring only if candy sticks, until the temperature reaches 238 degrees.

Remove from stove; add the butter, but do not stir. Keep the thermometer in the pan until the temperature goes down to 150 degrees.

Remove the thermometer, add the vanilla, and start beating until the candy loses its gloss and begins to feel grainy. Turn into buttered eight-inch-square pan and mark into squares.

Wrap in waxed paper or colorful tissue paper, fringing the ends.

SOURCE: Virginia Pasley, *The Holiday Candy Book*. Copyright © 1952 by Virginia Pasley. Reprinted by permission of Little, Brown and Co., in association with the Atlantic Monthly Press.

Presenting the Gifts

There is no more lovely custom than that of presenting gifts at Christmastime, a tradition brimming with poetry and sentiment. Everyone likes to give presents, everyone likes to receive them, and to the children, especially, Christmas should be made the merriest day of the year.

Parents' methods of giving gifts to their children varied slightly. Generally, however, Santa Claus brought the smaller gifts in the stocking and on the tree; but the larger ones, under the tree, were understood to come from "Mama and Papa."

Santa Claus has changed somewhat, through the years. In the United States, at least, he has always been seen as benevolent, leaving only an occasional peach-tree switch or piece of coal in a child's stocking. He became plumper and rounder than his European counterpart and was helped along in that direction by Thomas Nast and his drawings for *Harper's Bazaar* and *Harper's Weekly*. Clement Moore's *A Visit from Saint Nicholas* painted a word picture we still enjoy today.

Children hung their stockings on the mantelpiece or at the foot of their beds, to be filled with an orange, nuts, and smaller presents.

With the great economic suffering in the South during the Civil War, many families weren't able to celebrate Christmas as they had formerly. Many people weren't able to celebrate at all, but told their children that the Yankees had captured Santa Claus.[8]

In families of Dutch descent, the children of the household put carrots and straw in their wooden shoes and placed them by the hearth, along with a bucket of water for Saint Nicholas's horse.

The more important presents were opened after breakfast. Many gifts were hung on the tree, and the rest were placed under it. When the gifts were taken up and distributed, it gave the tree a rather bare look. The candy and cookies were not removed, however, until the tree was taken down.

The Victorians had many ways to distribute gifts and were always open to suggestions for still more novel ideas. A reader sent a letter to *Saint Nicholas* magazine, suggesting a novel way of distributing Christmas gifts for those who were "willing to depart from the good old customs of the Christmas Tree, the stocking hung by the chimney, and the 'Christmas Pie'." She sent these directions for the benefit of those who have never attended "cobweb parties."

Procure as many balls of string as there are members in the family. They should be different colors, so that each one may follow his string with ease, and of the same length, so that they all may finish winding together.

The presents intended for each person are to be tied to one particular string, the heaviest or largest to be fastened to one end and placed at the back of the room, set apart from the maze. Then carry the string across the room, tie something else to it, and secure the string to a chair, the window fastener, the curtain rod, or anything else.

Pass the string back and forth, up and down, through, behind, under, over, and across the furniture of the room in every conceivable manner, until the other end is reached, displaying as much as possible all light and attractive articles, while the heavier ones, of course, must rest on something solid. A number of little things, like scent sachets, lace bags tied with bright ribbon and filled with candy, and glittering cornucopias should be attached to the string as it is passed over the chandelier.

The hiding of small and valuable things, such as rings, pins, and other pieces of jewelry, thimbles, money, etc., under the sofa cushions, behind a book, or well concealed in any other way, gives additional interest to the maze, as the recipient comes upon them unexpectedly.

Proceed in a similar manner with the other strings, taking care as before to show the pretty things, to avoid snarls, and to make as many angles as you can.

The free ends of the strings should have spools or reels fastened to them, to wind the strings on as fast as disentangled, and should be placed near the door.

Mottoes or quotations referring to the gifts add to the fun when they are found just before seeing the objects to which they refer.

When all is ready, let the mistress of ceremonies precede the family, singing or saying the old song:
"Will you come into my parlor?"
Said the spider to the fly.
"'Tis the prettiest little parlor that ever you did spy;
The way into my parlor is up a winding stair,
And I have many pretty things to show you when you're there.
Will you, will you, walk in, Mister Fly?"
The door of the room should be opened just as the leader finishes the song, and after a short time for inspection he or she should place the reels in the hands of the right persons and bid them take all they find as they follow the threads through the labyrinth.[9]

This way of distributing gifts, while unusual, was not out of the ordinary, and you will find it mentioned again in the "Parties" chapter.

The "Christmas Pie," also known as "Bran Pie," mentioned in the letter was a device used to distribute family gifts and party favors as well, and had many variations.

"Bran" could have been any kind of grain. Any kind you find the least expensive will do, or if you object to using food in this way, sawdust may be substituted.

The simplest method is to use a large, deep, brown dish for the pie. Put a gift for everyone who will be at the Christmas dinner in the dish. Cover the gifts with bran, and put a sprig of holly in the center. After dinner, have the bran pie put on the table with a spoon and plates beside it, and invite everyone to take a portion, each spoonful bringing out whatever it touches. Funny little articles may be put in the pie, and the frequent inappropriateness of the gift to the receiver of it helps to create laughter.

A more sophisticated version with gifts earmarked specifically is done in this way: Cover the outside of a bowl or a new pie pan with pleated white tissue paper. Paste or tape the paper overlapping on the inside of the container, and on the bottom. Depending on the number of gifts you intend the pie to contain, cut a corresponding number of slits in a circular piece of white tissue paper that is to form the top crust.

(If that sounds like too much trouble, a large decorative bowl may be used as is, and a piece of brown paper glued to the top may act as a crust.)

Wrap each present in a bright-colored piece of tissue paper and tie with a narrow ribbon of the same color. Be sure to fasten the knot on top of the package securely, so there will be no possibility of its slipping from the parcel when it is jerked out of its bed of bran. Fill the pan with bran or sawdust, arrange the gifts on top in the order you wish, then put more bran over the parcels, heaping it in the center. Thread each ribbon through its respective slit in the cover and bring the cover cautiously down over the pie without tearing it. Gather the edge of the cover a little at a time with your fingers and paste it down over the sides. Glue a ribbon around the edge to cover the seam.

Give each person a color and let each pull in turn.

For a truly special gift, make a pie for one person, and attach a slip of paper to each ribbon with various hours written on them so the recipient may open presents from time to time during the day.

Puncture a small hole in the center of the top and insert a sprig of holly.[10]

One family told, in an 1895 issue of the *American Agriculturist*, of their decision to have "A Pillowcase Christmas."

A clothesline was brought in from the back yard and attached to two strong nails in opposite corners of the sitting room. For extra safety, another bit of rope was tied to the clothesline and fixed to a hook in the ceiling, to keep the line from sagging too much under the weight of such gifts as books and dishes and rubber boots. Then pillowcases were hung on the clothesline and labeled with the names of those who would receive gifts. Four clothespins fastened each pillowcase securely to the line, leaving the top open, so that gifts could be slipped inside.

The younger children went to bed early and the older children and parents filled the pillowcases and wrote appropriate poems for each gift. One little jingle said, "Here's an apron for Hattie, the dear little fatty."

When the pillowcases were filled, some were so heavy they dragged on the rope in places; others had handles poking out of the top and bulges everywhere.

The presents were opened after breakfast, which was eaten hurriedly, so that it could be cleared away and the presents brought in. The smallest person brought in the first pillowcase of gifts, and the others then followed. Gifts included warm, lined overshoes, volumes of Longfellow's poems, mother-of-pearl penholders, and many more items.[11]

The forerunner of today's gift-within-a-box-within-a-box is the "*Julklapp.*" Americans descending from Scandinavian stock favored this form of gift-giving. All the presents intended for *Julklapp* delivery must be prepared by enclosing them in wrappers of various kinds, the more unrelated to the contents, the better. For instance, a pretty trinket would be wrapped in fringed tissue paper, then in a small box, then in brown paper, then in strips of cloth until it was round like a ball. The ball would then be covered with dough and browned in the oven. It would then be pinned up in a napkin, and finally wrapped in white wrapping paper and string.[12]

For those interested in more traditional wrappings, tissue paper was the common wrapping material and was used in a variety of colors, tied with narrow ribbons.

"Miss Thoughtful," in *The Ladies' Home Journal* of December 1892, advises, "that while white paper may be used with any color ribbon, yellow paper should be wrapped in white, pink paper with blue, blue paper with pink, and red paper with gold ribbon."[13]

"A Rainbow Christmas" was described by Mrs. Scovil for her readers in *The Ladies' Home Journal* of December 1897. Her family, too, she wrote, had tired of the traditional way of giving gifts; and the old legend that "He who digs at the end of the rainbow, when it touches the earth, will find treasure," served as their inspiration. They made a "rainbow," of strong, unbleached cotton sheeting, with the inner part of the "bow" cut out and the upper corners above the "rainbow" left square to suspend it by and roughly painted in gray and black to represent storm clouds. The "bow" spanned a large window twelve feet wide, which nearly filled one end of the room. Bags of different colored silks, bright cottons, and cheesecloth held gifts and were suspended from the ends of the "rainbow," making a brilliant finish.[14]

19

Strands of Christmas "roping" embellished Victorian windows and curtains.

II Decorating the House

Victorian homes were made bright and cheerful for the Christmas holiday. The decorations for the house were as simple or as elaborate as the owner cared to make them; some did nothing more than place a green wreath at each window facing the street, while others made carefully wrought designs for the principal rooms.[1]

Choosing and collecting greens presented no problem for people living in the country and in small towns; they had only to go out into the fields and pick whatever was at hand. If they chose to make intricate designs of stars and crosses, as well as the customary wreaths, they had to fashion those, themselves.

There was no need to pity those living in the city, however, especially in New York, where the Washington Market sold just about everything, from turkeys and fish to fruit and vegetables and—just before Christmas—immense quantities of evergreens. There were great piles stacked in the streets and on the walks, and the whole neighborhood for a time had the fragrance of the forest. Shoppers could find large and small trees, short and long wreaths (roping was often called wreaths or wreathing), and readymade rings, crosses, stars, and many other devices.[2]

A Victorian parlor is beautified with greenery.

Winslow Homer's "Christmas: Gathering Evergreens" immortalizes seasonal search for greenery.

The evergreens most commonly used were hemlock, spruce, laurel, cedar, ground pine, and arbor vitae. Lycopodium is another name for ground pine. It may be ordered today from the florist; it is long-lasting and keeps its color well. This marvelous plant was also called *bouquet green*—obviously, it had as many names as it had uses. Ivy and ferns—especially those that had been pressed—were used profusely.[3] Hollies of all kinds were employed, especially for table decoration. Since holly was scarce in some areas, it was often massed for greater effect, rather than scattered about here and there. Smilax was used for trimming curtains, because it is so delicate and light in weight. Pressed ferns were also used in this way. Mistletoe, of course, accented the kissing bell (also known as the *kissing ball* or *bough*). In addition to the greens mentioned, others were used if they were common to the area.

A custom in the deep South in holiday decorating was the use of Spanish moss and magnolia leaves on the wall and the tablecloth, in addition to the usual holly and mistletoe.

While greens of all kinds are beautiful, *Vick's Floral Guide*, a thoroughly read magazine of the Victorian era, suggests in an 1879 issue that color should be added, to keep the decorations from looking like those used in a house of mourning. Mr. Vick proposed mixing decorations of autumn leaves with the greens.[4] Other writers agreed and suggested pressing fall leaves as soon as they began to change color.

These leaves may be pressed between sections of weighted-down newspapers or in old telephone books, both printed on paper more porous and absorbent than the glossy-finish paper in most magazines and catalogues. Press leaves of good color, free of blemishes, and put them in a warm, dry place during the drying period. After they are thoroughly dry, the leaves may be dipped into melted paraffin, which strengthens them, making them easier to handle. In this state, they can be pinned, sewed, or wired for use in decorating.

In addition to autumn leaves, grasses of all kinds add a light, airy touch. Everlastings, such as strawflowers, gomphrena, cockscomb, and statice, were especially welcomed by Victorian decorators, for their color and durability.[5] If you have not preserved any of your own, they are available in some flower and gift shops, or they can be ordered through the mail. (See "Sources".)

Grains were used, both in natural color and dyed. Often they were immersed overnight in a solution of alum and water until crystals formed.[6] A similar effect can be achieved by spraying the grains (also grasses and lunaria) with spray glue, then sprinkling with "diamond dust," while the glue is still wet. "Diamond dust" is white or colorless glitter, available in most craft shops.

To add color and interest to decorating projects, berries were collected in the fall. Mountain ash berries were preserved by packing them lightly in dry white sand in a wooden box in a cool, dry place, taking them out just before Christmas. Bittersweet, rose hips, and holly berries were hoarded, as well, and much prized for brightening the holiday.[7]

All sorts of designs may be created from the materials mentioned. Mottoes, letters, greetings, wreaths, and garlands were very popular; and if you attempt these, here's a word of encouragement from the editor of *Vick's*: "Festival decorations are not designed for close inspection, but for general effect, and simple materials may be used with the most satisfactory results."[8]

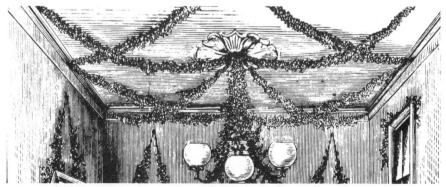

Criss-crossing a Victorian ceiling, garlands cascade downward at the light fixture.

23

*Strands of evergreen —probably ivy —trim a
picture frame and its hanger.*

*Hung vertically, instead of in festoons, roping
forms a decorative curtain.*

Garlands and wreaths were especially favored. If roping cannot be purchased or is too expensive, it can be easily made by using wire or strong
cord. [9] I prefer strong green cord. Tie one end to a door knob, or something
of about that height, so that the cord can be held taut. Cut short pieces of
evergreen (pine is often used); lay the stems along the cord and lash them to
the cord with fine wire (27-gauge is good—it comes on a roll and is available
at most hardware stores); place more pieces of greens slightly overlapping
the first and wire-wrap them in place, making the garland as full as you like.
If it seems fuller in some places than others, trim it with clippers instead of
taking it apart.

Roping was wrapped around posts, looped on stairways, attached to
overhead light fixtures and then stretched from the fixtures to the corners of
the room. It was also used as temporary picture frames or wrapped around
wires to look as if it were holding up a picture.

Green Wreath

Materials needed:
Masonite or cardboard
Glue
Assorted greens
Green plastic wrap or strips
  of dry-cleaner bags
Wire for hanger
Ribbon
Floral picks
Berries or other trims

Tools needed:
Saber saw for Masonite
Strong scissors for cardboard
Clippers

Wreaths were used alone or with garlands of roping, both inside and outside the house. My favorite method of making a green wreath is a very simple one:

Cut a circle of Masonite the size that suits your purpose best. A saber saw is necessary to cut out the inner circle. If a saber saw is not available, and the wreath will not be out in the weather, substitute cardboard for the base. Cut two pieces of cardboard and glue them together for strength. The most common size is twelve inches in diameter, with a three-inch center. The beauty of this wreath, aside from the ease with which it can be made, is that it can be cut into any size and shape desired.

Wrap the ring with plastic strips, using green plastic wrap from the florist, or dry cleaner bags doubled and cut into strips. Don't overlap them. When one strip ends, tie another to it, as the knots will not show on the finished wreath.

Many kinds of greens may be used for one wreath—including clippings from the shrubbery, since pieces need only be two or three inches long. The greens should be "hardened" before using, so the wreath will stay fresh. Harden greens by placing the stems in very warm water overnight.

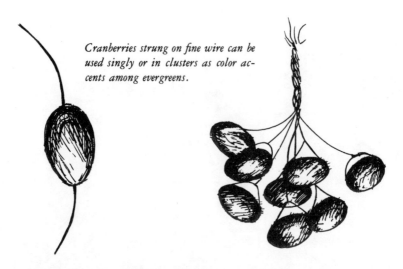

Cranberries strung on fine wire can be used singly or in clusters as color accents among evergreens.

After the ring is completely wound with plastic, tuck short pieces of greens into the plastic strips as if they were being tucked into a pocket — see drawing, page 25. Do one row, then the next, working your way around the wreath. Be generous with the greens; if they're skimpy, the wreath will not hold together. Twist a wire around the top of the frame for a hanger, and trim with small ribbon bows attached to floral picks, or with a large ribbon bow. Tuck berries here and there among the greens. If none of the berries mentioned earlier are available, cranberries may be strung on fine wire to form a cluster. Dried peas and beans softened (but not cooked) by boiling were put on wire by the Victorians in the same manner as the cranberries and given a scarlet coat by dipping them in sealing wax before making them into bunches. Red dye in paraffin, or melted red candles, will do as a substitute for sealing wax.

The Victorian method for making a green wreath was to lash small bunches of greens to a heavy wire frame, using fine-gauge wire to hold the greens in place. Their method is similar to shaping a metal coat hanger into a circle and wiring greens to it. This is a difficult method, in many ways, and I find the simpler Masonite wreath gives the same result, or better. The plan in this book is to show how the Victorians decorated their homes for Christmas, but substituting today's methods and materials. *Plastic is something that should never show, but is useful for underpinnings.*

A wreath may also be made by stuffing a purchased wire wreath form with damp sphagnum moss, wrapping it with florist's plastic wrap, and inserting the greens into the moss. Boxwood is generally used this way; it makes a heavy, long-lasting wreath.

Mottoes, Letters, and Greetings

Materials needed:
Mat board
Cotton (or polyester fiber)
Spray glue
Diamond dust
Gold paper, colored tissue paper
Crumpled tinfoil or
    aluminum foil
Velverette glue
Rice
Velveteen or red felt/flannel
Popcorn, strung
Gold spray paint
Gold paint (jar)
Waxed paper
Thread, string
Everlastings (straw
    flowers, etc.)
Treated greens
Wooden strips
Fine wire, on a spool
Staples

Tools needed:
Heavy scissors
Needle
Paintbrush
Staple gun

In addition to using greens in various ways, more permanent decorations were made; these often took the form of mottoes, letters, and greetings.

Mat board is a practical type of cardboard to use for the letters. It is strong, but not too thick to cut. Avoid corrugated cardboard—it is too flimsy. Mat board may be found at most art or stationery stores.

The words "Welcome," or "Peace On Earth," or the initials "I.H.S." (*Jesus Hominum Salvator*), as well as "Merry Christmas" and "A Happy New Year" were commonly used.

Determine the height of the letters you intend to use, marking them with a pencil; divide the height into six equal parts by drawing lines across the

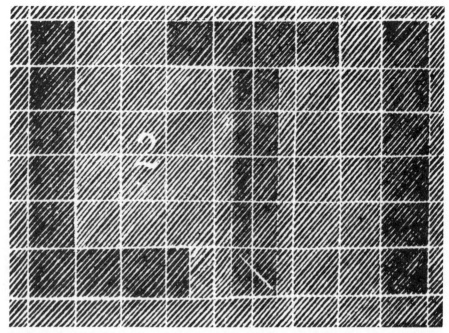

Block letters of any size can be made from patterns worked out on graph paper. One-inch squares are helpful starters.

board, as shown in the sketch. It is a good idea to work with one-inch squares. Four of these squares will be a good proportion for the width of most letters. The few letters that vary from that can be correctly made by the following arrangement: suppose the letters are six inches high; then four inches would be the proper width for B, C, D, H, N, O, P, Q, R, U, and Z; four-and-a-half inches wide for A, G, K, T, V, X, Y; the letter M should be five inches; W, six inches; E, F, L, three-and-a-half inches; J, three inches. With this arrangement, letters of any size can be made by simply dividing the height into six sections and using four as the average width. Try cutting the letters out of graph paper, then tracing around them onto the cardboard. These letters will be thin; but once they are covered with some material or other, they fatten up.

SOURCE: *Vick's Floral Guide*, December 1864.

Letters in various sizes are available in art and stationery stores. If you can find the right size, these letters may be used as patterns.

28

Very pretty letters are made by covering cardboard bases with cotton glued in place, then gently pulled until it is fluffy. Spray with spray glue and sprinkle with "diamond dust." The Victorians used glue and coarsely ground mica to gain this same effect. Letters were also covered with gold paper, colored tissue paper, or crumpled tinfoil (or aluminum foil, today), glued into place. Rice was also used to good advantage and gives a rich, unusual texture to the letters.[10] A thick glue such as "Velverette" should coat the letter form before the rice is sprinkled over all.

A beautiful letter can be made by covering cardboard with velveteen in some dark color like scarlet, olive, or blue. Fasten the cloth in place by folding the edges over the letter and sewing them on the back. String popped corn and tack it around the edges of the letter, fastening it well by taking stitches here and there through the cloth covering.

The popcorn may be left white, but it was thought that, when painted gold, it looked like coined or hammered metalwork.[11] In the 1800s, the popcorn was painted with gilding liquid; today, it is easier to spray the strings of popcorn with gold paint, attach them to the velveteen, then touch them up carefully here and there as needed with a little gold paint from a jar. Tuck a little waxed paper under the popcorn as you work, so that the paint won't drip onto the fabric. These letters are effective on dark or light backgrounds, as the gilding outlines them clearly and brings them out in proper light.

Letter forms may also be covered with everlastings, such as strawflowers, with the small spaces filled in with gomphrena or statice. Use a thick craft glue, such as "Velverette," for this.[12]

If letters are to be covered with greens, perhaps a sturdier foundation than cardboard should be used. In the past, laths were the suggested material for making letters of this weight, but since this building material is no longer available, good substitutes are yardsticks or screen molding, and some lumber yards will sell you something they call "lattice strips," which also works. Screen molding, as its name suggests, is used to make window screens and is a good size for making letters (three-quarters of an inch wide and one-quarter of an inch thick). The Victorians drilled holes into the wood and stitched small bunches of greens in place. If a long-lasting decoration is desired, treated lycopodium (dyed) may be used and is easily wired or stapled into place. The finished letters may be glued onto a string or ribbon to span a doorway or wall.

Holly Wreath

Materials needed:
Cardboard
Gold paper
Holly leaves
Red or green paint
Glue
Wire for hanger

Tools needed:
Scissors
Paintbrush

In addition to letters, more complicated designs may be made. Cut out a circle of cardboard to the desired size and cover it with light-blue paper or paint. The Victorians stitched their holly berries around the edge, but gluing would be easier. If you care to sew the berries and leaves on, holes should first be punched into the cardboard. The letters inside the wreath were of gold and brilliant colors pasted to the cardboard. Insert a wire in the wreath top for hanging.

SOURCE: *Harper's Young People,* 7 December 1880, p. 86.

Four-Sided Wreath

Materials needed:
Cardboard
Evergreens
Thread
Straw wreaths
Strapping tape
Lath-type wood
Nails
Styrofoam
Wire
Fern pins
Staples
Pressed ferns
Glue
Berries

Tools needed:
Darning needle (optional)
Needle (optional)
Saw or sharp knife
Hammer
Staple gun

For this interestingly shaped wreath, the Victorians used cardboard perforated with a darning needle, so that the greens could be stitched into place. The evergreen suggested here was lycopodium, since it is light-weight and pliable and available fresh or treated and dyed. The color of the preserved greens is somewhat darker than a natural green, but it does make a more permanent wreath than the fresh greens, so I find it useful. This wreath does take some time to make, so for that reason, as well, I feel it should be made with long-lasting material.

Instead of using cardboard as a base, try substituting two straw wreaths; these are commonly found in variety stores and plant and flower shops and are often wrapped in green plastic. Remove the plastic wrapping and cut the wreaths in half with a saw or a sharp knife; but before making the cut, wrap each side of the place to be cut with strapping tape, so the wreath will not unravel. Attach the halves at each corner with pieces of narrow wood (screen molding, yardsticks, etc.) nailed into place; and for futher reinforcement, glue a triangle of styrofoam and wrap with strapping tape.

Cut a cardboard crescent as shown in the sketch. Poke two small holes into it; put wires into them and wire to the wreath.

Add a wire to the top of the wreath for hanging.

Using straw wreaths makes a plumper wreath than the cardboard does. Small greens such as boxwood, lycopodium, or holly may be attached to the straw wreath with fern pins, or with long staples from a staple gun.

After the wreath is completely covered, except for the crescents, cover them with sprays of hemlock, arbor vitae, and pressed ferns and grasses held in place with glue or staples. Hide the stems with pressed ivy leaves and artificial berries glued into place.

This wreath may hang on its own or as a surround for the letters mentioned earlier.

SOURCE: *Harper's Young People*, 7 December 1880, p. 86.

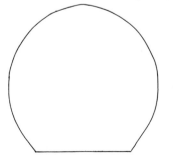

A cardboard crescent is used in making the four-sided wreath at left and above. Two wires fix the crescent to the wreath. (See Appendix A for full-sized pattern.)

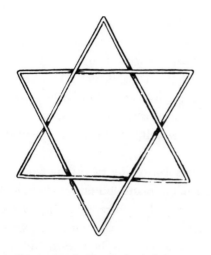 

A Decorated Six-Pointed Star

Materials needed:
Wood screen molding
Nail
Staples
Fine wire on a spool
Treated lycopodium
Hot glue

Everlastings or paper flowers
Tools needed:
Saw
Hammer
Staple gun
Glue gun

This wall design of a hexagonal star was found in an 1888 issue of *The Ladies' Home Journal*. It was constructed of thin strips of wood with the pieces nailed, wired, or stapled where they intersect. Wood called screen molding—or lattice strips, if you can find them—is a good size and weight—three-quarters of an inch wide and one-quarter of an inch thick.

Small pieces of evergreens may be lashed to these wooden pieces with fine-gauge spool wire; or if treated lycopodium is used, it may be stapled in place or held in place with hot glue from a glue gun. The glue gun works well with light-weight materials.

After the star is completely covered with greens, a cluster of flowers may be wired onto each intersection, for color. The flowers may be everlastings, such as strawflowers, or small paper flowers, so long as they have wire stems so that they may be attached to the star.

A little nosegay in the center adds to the whole design and may be attached by fine wires extending from the four intersections, as shown in the sketch.

SOURCE: *The Ladies' Home Journal*, December 1888, p. 14.

A Christmas Harp

Materials needed:
Light-weight wood
　or heavy cardboard
Colored leaves
Wire
Berries
Glue

Tools needed:
Saw
Heavy scissors

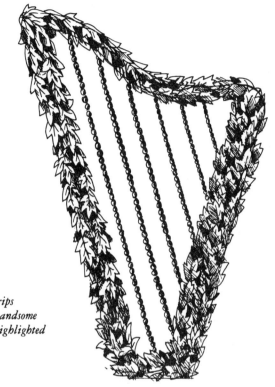

Stylized versions of musical instru-
ments made of cardboard or wood strips
covered with dried fall leaves were handsome
Victorian space-fillers. Red berries highlighted
the wire "strings."

The Christmas harp described here was shown in the *American Agricul-turist* for December 1879. In giving instructions for making it, the writer advised the reader to take into consideration where the harp was to be placed. If it was to be put above a mantel, it needed to be rather small; if it was to be a part of the decorations of a large hall, then it should be enlarged accordingly.

The frame of the harp can be made of heavy cardboard or light-weight wood, and the strings of fine wire. However, if the harp is to be made quite large, the strings show up much better if they're made of wood, and wooden "strings" give the frame more stability. Assuming that wire will be used for the strings, string berries and attach the ends of the wires to the cardboard frame.

Cover the frame with colorful fall leaves glued into place.

The harp may lean against a wall or a piece of furniture; or two wires may be attached to each corner for hanging.

Source: *American Agriculturist*, December 1879, p. 510.

33

A Lyre of Leaves

Materials needed:
Light-weight wood or
heavy cardboard
Colored leaves
Wire
Berries
Glue

Tools needed:
Saw
Heavy scissors

The design for this decoration, inspired by an ancient lyre, was also featured in the same issue of the *American Agriculturist* that showed the Christmas harp. The lyre is made in generally the same way. As shown in the sketch, the strings are fewer than those needed for the harp and therefore may be made broader, so strips of wood or cardboard may be used, with the berries strung in double rows on the string front, or the berries can be glued directly onto the strip.

SOURCE: *American Agriculturist*, December 1879, p. 510.

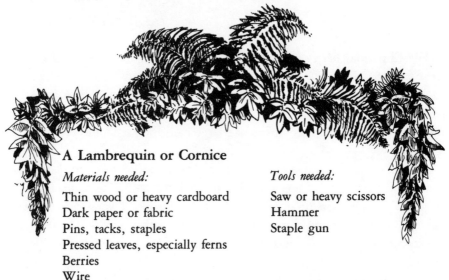

A Lambrequin or Cornice

Materials needed:
Thin wood or heavy cardboard
Dark paper or fabric
Pins, tacks, staples
Pressed leaves, especially ferns
Berries
Wire

Tools needed:
Saw or heavy scissors
Hammer
Staple gun

The *American Agriculturist* for December 1881 suggests the lambrequin as a decoration for the windows or to be used above a picture or mirror.

If the cornice is to be placed above a window, a strong support will be

34

needed, since the length will be greater. Cut light-weight cardboard to the right size to act as a frame for the window; affix wires so that the cardboard may be attached to the window frame. Cover the cardboard with paper or fabric, so that the leaves may be easily attached to the cornice, using pins or staples (using staple gun) or both.

If the decoration is for a picture or a mirror, heavily starched fabric is suggested, cut into the same shape as the space it will occupy. Spread the fabric or the cardboard out on a table and cover with fall leaves, pressed ferns, and everlastings. The ferns must be pressed, or they will curl up, as they dry out, and become shapeless. (Instructions for pressing may be found on pages 22–23.) They may be pinned, stapled, or stitched into place. Follow the general design in the sketch.

Source: *American Agriculturist*, December 1881, p. 531.

Banners

Materials needed:
Heavy fabric (felt)
Evergreens
Glue
Thread
Paint (water colors
—optional)
Felt-tipped pen
Dowel
Ribbon
Tools needed:
Scissors
Needle
Paintbrush
(optional)

Banners are a great help in decorating for Christmas and are a change from the usual wreaths and roping. They also have the added advantage of being permanent, so they can be kept from year to year.

The sketches shown here were adapted from the *American Agriculturist* for December 1881 and may be used as a guide in proportioning the banner. The bottoms may be straight across or as they are shown here.

Banners may be made of any common material. Felt would be suggested for use today, since it is easy to work with, hangs well, is readily available, and comes in a variety of colors. The color considered most effective was red or any other warm color, and the edging was to be made of green ribbon or another green material. The lettering may be cut from fabric and glued in place, or painted on in water colors. A simpler method would be to use a felt-tipped pen; but experiment, first, to see whether that is the medium easiest for you.

When you have decided on the size, cut your banner to the desired shape, using the sketch as a guide. Stitch a hem at the top just large enough to slip a dowel through. Attach a ribbon for hanging and bows at each end, as shown.

SOURCE: *American Agriculturist*, December 1881, p. 531.

Kissing Bells

Materials needed:	Potato
Mistletoe	Thread
Evergreens	Ribbon
Excelsior	Plastic berry boxes
Sheet moss	Oasis or Filfast
Fresh ferns	Foil
Wooden floral picks	*Tools needed:*
Treated ferns (optional)	Clippers

"Kissing bells" made of a variety of evergreens were placed in Victorian doorways throughout the Christmas season. These decorations were also called "kissing boughs" or "kissing balls." (See color section, Plate 1.)

One uncommon suggestion for making them was to mold excelsior the size of an apple, cover it with sheet moss, and wire fresh ferns to wooden picks pushed into the ball, completely covering it—then suspend it on a heavy black thread. Fresh ferns curl as they dry in the air, so the ferns on any ornament made that way would have to be kept damp by spraying them with water.

There are treated ferns on the market that would serve the same purpose; but if they are used, make the bell far in advance, because treated ferns give off an unpleasant odor and should be aired before hanging in an occupied room.

An easy-to-make and long-lasting kissing ball may be made by wiring two plastic berry boxes together with a piece of wet floral foam, such as Oasis or Filfast, between. For greater strength, the foam may be wrapped in foil. Push short pieces of hardened greens into the foam, with some long pieces here and there for interest, and a piece of mistletoe and red ribbon underneath. *Since fresh mistletoe loses its berries very quickly, artificial berries are recommended.*

Suspend the ball on a wire wrapped in ribbon.

Greens may also be inserted into a raw potato, which helps to keep them fresh. Wrap a wire around the potato as if it were a package, to strengthen it, leaving one end free for hanging. Position mistletoe and a ribbon bow underneath; then insert short pieces of evergreens, completely covering the potato.

Source: H. T. Williams, *The Ladies' Floral Cabinet* (New York: H. T. Williams, 1884), p. 395.

Decorated Bells

Materials needed:
Graduated hoops (optional)
Wire (optional)
Muslin (optional)
Fabric for lining
Styrofoam bell

Dried flowers
Leaves (optional)
Glue or pins
Tools needed:
Scissors

Decorated bells were hung in Victorian doorways and over tables, during the Yuletide holidays. These decorations were originally made of three graduated hoops wired together and covered with muslin. An easier method is to purchase a styrofoam bell and cover the inside with fabric and the outside with everlastings, either glued or pinned into place.

In Plate 11 (color section), the red bell over the table is made of dried cockscomb glued onto the styrofoam bell with Velverette glue; the lining is red satin, also glued in place, with Sobo glue.

A lovely bell may also be made of overlapping green leaves held in place with glue or pins.

A word of caution was given to the housewives in the 1800s about Christmas decorating: it was suggested that the decorations be confined to one room, such as the parlor or sitting room, because—although they *are* beautiful—decorations of Christmas greenery require constant supervision with a broom and dustpan. That was not necessarily a universal opinion, however; others suggested bringing in small live trees to be placed in the hall and on the stairs. Pots of ivy were placed where the ivy could trail around the pictures and windows. Poinsettias and other blooming plants decorated windows and conservatories and everything blended together to give the Victorian house a "Christmasy" look.[14]

Following European tradition, the American Victorian tree was originally arranged on a table instead of on the floor.

III The Christmas Tree

The Christmas tree is the most visible outward sign of the inward spirit of Christmas. The American Victorian tree was developed by the combined—and varied—influences of economic circumstance, taste, geographical location, and family heritage.

Stories of the first trees seen in the United States are many, beginning with tales of the trees prepared by the Hessian soldiers during the Revolutionary War; this is undocumented, but we do know that the Christmas tree is Germanic in origin. Queen Victoria's consort Prince Albert is often given credit for bringing the Christmas tree to England, but in truth he made popular a custom already practiced by other members of the British royal family.

Once middle-class Victorians were acquainted with the tree as illustrated and described in *The Illustrated London News* in 1848, they took it to their hearts—English and Americans alike. The Christmas tree eventually became even more popular in this country than it was in England, because of the availability here of evergreens.

Prince Albert's Christmas Tree was annually prepared, by command of Her Majesty Queen Victoria, for the royal children. The tree chosen for this purpose was a young fir about eight feet high, with six tiers of branches. On each branch, dozens of candles were arranged. Hanging from the branches were elegant trays, baskets, and other receptacles for candies of the most varied and expensive kinds, in all forms and colors. Fancy cakes, gilt gingerbread, and eggs filled with sweetmeats were hung from the branches by variously colored ribbons. The tree stood on a table covered with white damask; it was supported at the root by piles of toys and dolls. At the top of the tree stood the small figure of an angel, with outstretched wings, holding a wreath in each hand.

In 1850 Charles Dickens painted this word picture in *A Christmas Tree*.

I have been looking on, this evening, at a merry company of children assembled round that pretty German toy, a Christmas Tree. The tree was planted in the middle of a great round table, and towered high above their heads. It was brilliantly lighted by a multitude of little tapers; and everywhere sparkled and glittered with bright objects. There were rosy-cheeked dolls, hiding behind green leaves; and there were real watches (with moveable hands, at least, and an endless capacity for being wound up) dangling from innumerable twigs; there were French polished tables, chairs, bedsteads, eight-day clocks, and various other articles of domestic furniture (wonderfully made in tin) perched among the boughs, as if in preparation for some fairy housekeeping; there were jolly, broad-faced little men, much more agreeable in appearance than many real men—and no wonder, for their heads took off and showed them to be full of sugarplums; there were fiddles and drums, there were tambourines, books, work boxes, paint boxes, there were trinkets for the elder girls, far brighter than any grown-up gold and jewels; there were baskets and pincushions in all devices; there were guns, swords, and banners, there were witches standing in enchanted rings of pasteboard, to tell fortunes; there were teetotums, humming tops, needle cases, pen wipers, smelling bottles, conversation cards, bouquet holders, real fruit, made artificially dazzling with gold leaf; imitation gold leaf; imitation apples, pears, walnuts crammed with surprises; in short, as a pretty child before me delightedly whispered to another pretty child, her bosom friend, "there was everything and more."[1]

These Victorian Christmas trees may have been English, but their descriptions were carried in American magazines and served as a guide for decorating the American tree, as well. We can see by the long lists of decorations that the theme of the Victorian tree anywhere was "everything and more."

Traditionally, European Christmas trees were—and still are—placed on tables. The first published account of a tree being placed on the floor was given in *Godey's Lady's Book* of 1860.[2] The engraver, however, did not choose to go along with the text; as the reproduction of that illustration shows (see page 38), the American tree is not on the floor and bears a close resemblance to Prince Albert's tree.

Christmas eve was tree-trimming time; and in most houses, that pleasant activity was left to the parents and older children. Putting the tree in place was called "planting the tree"; the decorating of it was called "dressing the tree."

The same Christmas issue of *Godey's Lady's Book* that carried the Christmas tree engraving ran a story about the Christmas customs of a widowed doctor and his family.

On Christmas eve, according to the story—which was fiction, of course, based on idealized observance of prevailing customs—the doctor and his eldest daughters placed a green cloth in the center of the floor in their front parlor. A large stone jar filled with damp sand was placed on the cloth. The sand held the tree erect, even though the tree was so tall it almost reached the high ceiling. A flounce of green chintz concealed the jar; and around the top, a cushion of moss covered the sand.

The tree was garlanded with bright red holly berries on cord, festooned from the boughs. The doctor arranged tiny candles with long pieces of wire passing through the taper at the bottom; these wires clasped over the stem of each branch and twisted together underneath, and great care was taken to allow a clear space above each wick.

Small bouquets of paper flowers, strings of beads, tiny flags of gay ribbons, stars and shields of gilt paper, and lace bags filled with colored candies decorated the tree, all of them, along with knots of bright ribbon, making a brilliant show for a small amount of money.

In addition to the ornaments, the tree was decorated with presents. A basketwork of ribbon was formed to hold the most cumbersome gifts, which included dolls, a toy cart with toy horses, a workbasket, and a bird cage.

On Christmas morning, the doctor lit the candles while the younger children waited outside the closed doors. When all the candles were lighted, the children dashed in, with squeals of delight. The candles were set alight only on Christmas morning and perhaps once or twice again for parties. A bucket, holding a stick with a sponge on one end, was placed behind the tree in case of fire.[3]

Peterson's Magazine of December 1888 suggests that the children make many of the ornaments, most of which are of paper. (Directions for many of them are given at the end of this chapter.)[4]

Early magazine accounts of Christmas trees describe fir trees placed in a tub, held steady by stones, with paper covering the tub and moss placed over the stones. Under the tree a little garden or farm was placed. This was to create a scene of paper, moss, minerals, shells, and toy animals, with a landscape laid in from scraps of evergreens and looking glasses or silver paper for lakes and rivers. A fence, with palings cut out of paper, and walls of tiny twigs and stones often surrounded the panorama. The Pennsylvania Dutch called such a Christmas-tree yard a *"Putz."*[5]

Children were urged to create paper chains or thread red berries into garlands. Paper roses were intermixed with stars, hearts, and other designs threaded on long strands. Fairy figures added greatly to the beauty of the tree; cornucopias of all kinds were made, to hold candy and nuts. Gilded walnuts and acorns formed into bunches added sparkle.

Not all Victorian Christmases were bountiful and brimming with goodies: our next glimpse into the past does not reflect royalty, or even a middle-class holiday celebration, but shows us, through the eyes of a child, a Christmas spent in an army garrison during a very bad winter. The story appeared in the December 1892 issue of *Harper's Young People*.

A young boy wrote to a friend, explaining that the family had made everything, themselves, that year, in the way of tree ornaments and presents. Everyone was remembered, grown people as well as children. One man received a ginger-cake doll, and the boy's father got a pair of moccasins. One of the soldiers proved clever and inventive; he had made a complete set of doll's furniture—parlor, bedroom, and dining room—for the boy's sister and had made the letter-writer a baseball. In addition, he had obtained a lot of new tin from the quartermaster and cut it in thin strips, which curled as they were cut, and they had hung these tin strips on the tree, where they shone "as bright and pretty as real things you buy in a store." The soldier had also made a lot of decorative little flags of silk. Everyone joined in stringing popcorn, and one of the officers took some glue and ground mica and decorated apples and nuts so that they looked as if they were covered with frost. These, too, were hung on this beautiful homespun tree.

Decorating a really tall tree is a challenge, whether it was done in the last century or this one. Every year since 1976, the Office of Horticulture at the Smithsonian Institution has mounted the "Trees of Christmas Exhibit." Fifteen trees of all shapes and sizes are featured. My project has always been the American Victorian Christmas Tree, which is traditionally fourteen feet tall. The top branches must be reached by ladders pushed into the tree, so it has been thought best to put on the garlands, such as paper chains and popcorn, first, and then go back, adding the more fragile ornaments.

A writer in the 1800s suggested, instead, that, if one were using a tall tree, one should decorate the upper branches before setting up the tree, in case there were no ladders tall enough to reach the highest boughs. She felt that that could be managed by tying balls of white cotton batting on the tips of the branches, along with strings of cranberries, glittering ornaments, and so on; then, after setting the tree in place, other decorations that would "insure a brilliant effect" could be added. That could best be done, she felt, by avoiding bundles done up in brown paper, but instead using dolls, brightly colored books, toys, bright silk handerchiefs, sleds, and wagons and placing them, without wrappings, in prominent view.[6]

Reproducing the American Victorian Tree

Balsam and Douglas firs were widely used as Christmas trees in Victorian times in America, but whatever tree is common to your area is the one to choose first. In Victorian times, if a family lived in the country, they cut their own, but the markets in the cities carried a ready supply of trees and greens.

Christmas-tree holders as we know them today were uncommon;[7] most people resorted to wooden cross-pieces weighted down with stones and covered the base with a white sheet, using flannel or cotton batting to simulate snow. The jars and pots described previously were also used to hold the tree, and embellished with skirts or moss. Avoid the Christmas tree skirt covered with sequins—it wouldn't be authentic.

Garlands not only enhance the beauty of a tree, but help to reshape it through optical illusion if the tree is less than perfect.

Strings of popcorn may be tedious to make, but they are wonderfully decorative and, if stored carefully in mothballs, may be kept from year to year. Use strong thread, a sharp needle, and stale popcorn, keeping the strings in three-foot lengths to prevent tangling.

Holly berries and cranberries make colorful garlands. The Pennsylvania Dutch made strings of dried apple quarters. Tinsel is, of course, the gaudiest garland of all and became popular in this country in the late 1800s. Like most ornaments, it too originated in Germany. Try to use tinsel (either silver or gold) that is no more than an inch in diameter; today's tinsel is twice the size of the old-fashioned variety and, besides overpowering the other decorations on the tree, is not authentic; perhaps a trim might be in order.

Paper chains are easy to make, inexpensive, and, as *Godey's Lady's Book* says, "furnish much fun by the fireside" and can be easily made by children.[8]

Candles in metal holders were the most common method of lighting the tree; but in some wealthier city dwellings, glass pots holding oil were used.[9] Authentic metal holders and candles are being reproduced today (see "Sources") and although the candles should not be burned, they make a fine showing, especially with an unobtrusive spotlight shining on the tree.

43

Paper Ornaments

Materials needed:
Tracing paper
Cardboard
Bright, shiny paper
Glue
Yarn

Tools needed:
Scissors

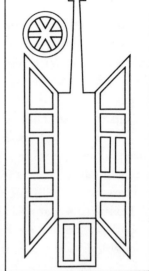

Ornament at far right can be either a sledge or a haywagon, depending on the way side pieces and back are folded. (See Appendix A, Patterns.)

Godey's Lady's Book of 1880 suggests making stars, hearts, crescents, harps, anchors, axes, and pitchers out of bright and shiny paper. See outlines from the book on pages 130–131. Trace them; then cut a pattern out of cardboard. For a more spectacular array of color, stars may be made one color on one side with another color glued to the back, with red or yellow yarn sandwiched in between, connecting stars and moons and whatever designs suit your fancy, guided by those shown here.

A butterfly can be easily made by cutting wings of one color with pasted-on spots of brown or black, with a second wing of another color pasted on the underside. The wings may be folded up and the body tied to the tree.

Red hearts make a bright showing, as does a golden axe with a scarlet handle.

The gold chariot on scarlet runners is a little more complicated, but not really difficult.

The magazine proposes saving these ornaments from year to year and suggests making them together as a family, stressing the sentiment that "It means laying up a fund of bright memories to be recalled in later years, when the home circle may be perhaps dispersed forever."

Source: *Godey's Lady's Book,* December 1880, p. 556.

44

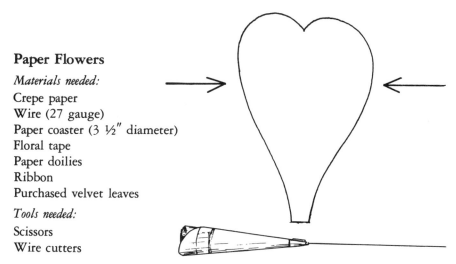

Paper Flowers

Materials needed:

Crepe paper
Wire (27 gauge)
Paper coaster (3 ½″ diameter)
Floral tape
Paper doilies
Ribbon
Purchased velvet leaves

Tools needed:

Scissors
Wire cutters

Florists' tape, wire, and crepe-paper petals make charming roses for a Victorian tussy-mussy, or hand bouquet. (See pattern, page 133.)

Crepe paper roses may be used individually or in bunches. If they are grouped together, surrounded by leaves or a paper collar or both, they may be called by the Victorian name *tussy-mussy*. A tussy-mussy, as the Victorians knew, was a hand bouquet, usually made of fresh or dried flowers. Today's dictionaries offer scant information on the term. Both the *Compact Edition of the Oxford English Dictionary* (1971) and *Webster's Third New International . . . Unabridged* (1971) do comment: *Webster's* says it is derived from Middle English *tusmose*, *tussemose*, a garland of flowers; the OED says the early form is *tus-* or *tussemose*, "a cluster or knot of flowers." Anyway, the Victorians made tussy-mussies for Christmas decorations, and instead of using dried or fresh flowers, they often made them of paper.

Using the pattern on page 133, cut fifteen petals with the grain of the paper. Wind one petal around a wire stem; tape about a fourth of the petal to the wire with floral tape to hold it securely. Cup the rest of the petals by pulling slightly at arrow points; then arrange four petals around the stem, overlapping each halfway; tape into place. Continue with the next row, alternating the petals as you tape. When the rose is the size you desire, push the wire stem through a paper doily coaster. Tape the wire underneath the doily to hold it in place. Add a ribbon bow with streamers.

A tussy-mussy may be made by grouping five or six roses together, perhaps taping a leaf to a stem here and there. Use a larger paper doily for a collar, tape in place, add ribbon bow and streamers.

SOURCE: Caroline L. Smith, *American Home Book of Indoor Games* (Boston: Lee and Shepard, Publishers, 1874).

Paper Chains

Materials needed:

Colored paper (construction
    paper, etc.)
Glue (Elmer's, Sobo)

Tools needed:

Scissors

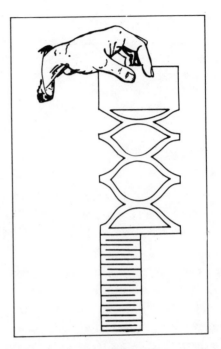

*Simple enough for children to make,
pretty enough to please everyone, paper
chains are standby make-it-yourself
decorations. This one is authentically
Victorian.*

Long paper chains fastened at the top of the tree and then allowed to droop in irregular festoons from branch to branch are easy to make.

The chain pictured here is made by taking a long strip of paper, two-and-a-half inches wide, and doubling it sharply down the middle. Then cut alternately from each side of the strip, always taking care not to cut quite to the farthest edge of the strip. When the strip is unfolded, there will be a delicate chain of fragile loops.

The paper for this chain should be the same color on both sides.

SOURCE: *Godey's Lady's Book*, December 1880, p. 555.

Simple Link Chain

The materials needed are the same as for the chain mentioned above, except that paper colored on one side only may be used for this chain.

Cut strips of paper four inches long and one inch wide. Overlap and glue one end slightly over the other, forming a link. Slip the next piece of paper through the link, gluing that and forming two links; continue in this way until the chain is the length you wish it.

Gold foil paper may be used for a bright effect.

SOURCE: Smith, *American Home Book of Indoor Games*.

46

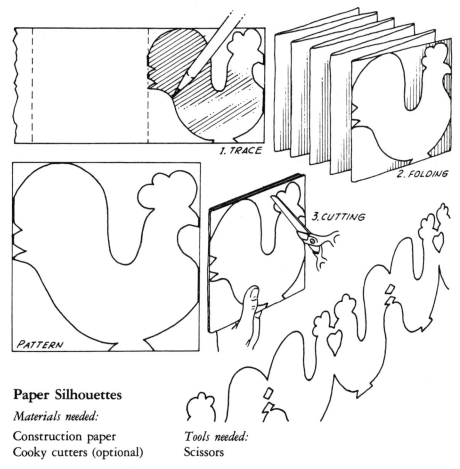

1. TRACE

2. FOLDING

3. CUTTING

PATTERN

Paper Silhouettes

Materials needed:

Construction paper
Cooky cutters (optional)

Tools needed:
Scissors

Decide which figure you want to make. It can be a string of animals, such as bears or elephants, or a set of figures, such as angels or snowmen. Fold the construction paper into several layers wide enough to accommodate the figure you have chosen and thick enough to make the chain the length you desire. On the folded construction paper, trace the pattern given or draw around your favorite cooky cutter.

Cut out the figure, being careful to leave part of the folded area on each side of the shape intact. If the folds are cut through entirely, the figures will not form a chain and will instead be separate and unattached to one another.

After the cutting is completed, open the paper figures and find a chain to surround the tree!

SOURCE: Design by Judith W. Blood, in *Christmas Decorations from Williamsburg's Folk Art Collection* (Williamsburg, Va.: Colonial Williamsburg Foundation, Publishers, 1976), p. 60. (Distributed by Holt, Rinehart & Winston.)

Paper Fans

Materials needed:
Construction paper or
    gold or silver wrapping papers

Ribbon and/or lace
Glue
Fine wire, for hanging

Tools needed:
Scissors
Stapler

Paper fans can be made any size, depending on the tree to be decorated. For fans to decorate most Christmas trees, a piece of construction paper cut in half, making it 4½ by 6 inches would be about the right size. Glue a ribbon lengthwise across the paper, about 1 inch from the top. After the glue is dry, fold the fan into accordian pleats ½-inch wide. While the fan pleats are still flattened, fold up 1 inch on the bottom and staple.

Glue a ribbon with streamers to the bottom of the fan, covering the staples.

The fan can be propped in the tree after it is opened, or may hang from a fine wire attached near the top. See color section, Plate 4.

SOURCE: *American Agriculturist*, December 1884, p. 549.

Tinsel Ornaments

Materials needed:
Narrow tinsel or wired tinsel
Fine wire
Masking tape

Reproductions of Victorian Santas,
    dolls, or scenes
Tools needed:
Scissors

"Keepsake" tree ornaments of old cards or Christmas scenes were popular with Victorians. Pictures were glued to a cardboard backing, with loops of tinsel for glitter and a thin wire for hanging.

Light-weight cardboard ornaments trimmed with tinsel were bought or made by the Victorians and are easily reproduced today.

The cards in the drawings show Santas, but many subjects were used: dolls, snow scenes, Christmas trees, and so on.

If you are not able to find narrow tinsel already wired, wrap fine (27-gauge) wire around narrow tinsel to give it body. To make sure it is held securely, tape tinsel loops to the wrong side of the card and glue another piece of light-weight cardboard to the back, covering the tape.

The card may be hung by a tinsel loop, if that is feasible, or a fine wire may be inserted into the ornament to be used as a hanger.

SOURCE: Snyder, *The Christmas Tree Book*, p. 61.

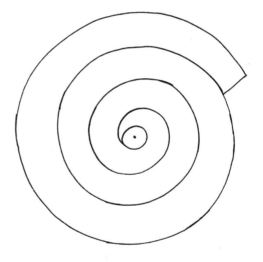

A Cardboard Snake

Materials needed:

Light-weight gold cardboard
Pin or fine wire

Tools needed:

Scissors

A snake of light-weight gold cardboard is a slightly different shape from most of the ornaments we've discovered and is certainly easy to make.

Using the sketch as a guide, cut a circle; then cut round and round until, when the center is held, the rest drops, to resemble a snake.

The center may be pinned or wired to a branch.

SOURCE: *Peterson's Magazine*, December 1880.

Scrap Ornaments

Materials needed:

Reproductions of antique paper
   dolls, angels, and Santa Clauses
Cotton (batting and polyester fiber)
Glue (Sobo)

Ribbon, lace, feathers, other
   fabric trims

Tools needed:

Scissors

Scrap pictures were very much admired by the Victorians. These scrap pictures were made for scrapbooks or were made as paper dolls or advertising give-aways.

They were hung on the tree as is, or could be dressed by gluing ribbon, lace, and feathers in place, especially in the case of the paper dolls. Some of these are being reproduced today. (See "Sources".)

If angels had clouds attached to them, the clouds were often made to look more fluffy by the addition of cotton glued in place. A Santa Claus was given a fluffy cotton beard.

SOURCE: Snyder, *The Christmas Tree Book*, p. 137.

Santa body:
6½ inches tall.

Cotton Ornaments

Materials needed:

Cardboard
Cotton batting
Fluffy cotton (or polyester fiber)
Glue (Sobo or Elmer's)

Seals or faces cut out of greeting
   cards, or paper
Thread for hanger

Tools needed:

Scissors

The cotton ornaments in the sketch (page 50) were inspired by those imported from Germany in the 1800s and pictured in Phillip V. Snyder's book *The Christmas Tree Book*. Cut out a face or a figure from wrapping paper or an old Christmas card — it doesn't matter which, so long as the picture reflects our period. Make a cardboard backing for it. The Santa was made by gluing a seal to a piece of cardboard, then covering the whole with a strip of cotton lapped over in the front. The arms are made by rolling cotton batting, then gluing in place. Add red felt mittens and small twigs or dried-leaf stems for switches.

Glue a string hanger on the back. Add a strip around the head, and the fluffier cotton for the beard.

The lady was made in much the same way, except that she was cut out of wrapping paper. A cardboard backing was made; then pieces of cotton were glued to resemble fur circling her neck, sleeves, muff, and skirt.

Cotton batting strips were often laid along the tree branches to simulate snow. Cotton balls were touched with glue and ground mica. We can substitute spray glue and diamond dust to get the same effect.

Source: Snyder, *The Christmas Tree Book*, p. 54.

Cornucopias

Materials needed:
Lightweight cardboard
Gold and silver paper
Aluminum foil
Ribbon
Paper doily
Decorative seals
Ice cream cone

Tools needed:
Scissors
Small pick
Stapler

Many cornucopias were made of colored lightweight cardboard decorated with a seal, with perhaps a ribbon around the top with a loop for a hanger.

Use the sketch shown as a pattern; cut the cardboard and overlap about a quarter of an inch, gluing one side over the other. Hold in place for a few minutes until the glue takes hold. Add trim. Fill with candy and nuts for the tree.

The same cornucopia may be covered with gold or silver paper, or an ice cream cone can be covered with aluminum foil. Punch holes on either side of the cone near the top, insert a ribbon through the holes to use as a hanger. Add a ribbon around the top, a seal on the front, and it's finished. If seals with the proper Victorian flavor are not obtainable, look for wrapping paper. (See "Sources".)

A paper doily can be turned into a cornucopia in no time. Fold a nine- or ten-inch doily so that as much "lace" as possible shows. Wrap it around your hand until it becomes a a cone shape, about the size of an ice cream cone. Don't make it too fat; most Victorian cones were thinner, rather than fatter than our ice cream cones. Staple or glue the seam, affix a decorative seal in place, as shown. Glue on a ribbon hanger with side bows.

SOURCE: Smith, *The American Home Book of Indoor Games.*

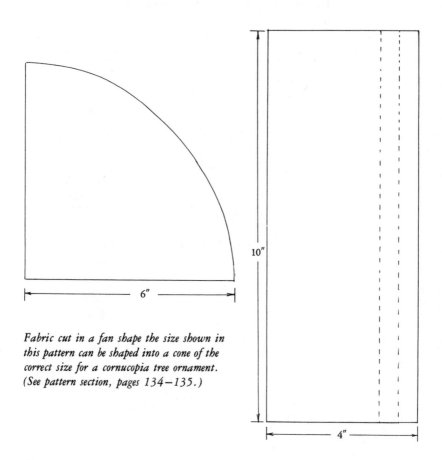

Fabric cut in a fan shape the size shown in this pattern can be shaped into a cone of the correct size for a cornucopia tree ornament. (See pattern section, pages 134–135.)

Fabric Ornaments

Cornucopias

Materials needed:
Lightweight cardboard
Fabric
Ribbon
Glue
Lace

Tools needed:
Scissors

To make a cornucopia with a fabric top, cut out a light-weight piece of cardboard for the bottom; glue along the straight edge and overlap about a half-inch.

For the top, cut fabric according to the pattern on page 135; turn wrong sides together and seam about a half-inch inside the fabric. Turn down about an inch from the top to make a casing for the drawstring. Turn to the right side. Glue the bottom of the fabric (unfinished part) to the top of the cone, overlapping slightly. After the glue is dry, cover this seam with trim.

Add ribbon through casing. This will serve as a hanger.

A simpler method is to cut the cone from heavy upholstery fabric, again using the sketch as a guide. Cut a piece of lace the length specified in the pattern and topstitch it to the round part of the piece of fabric. Turn wrong side out and make one long seam, starting at the top of the lace and going down to the point of the cone. Turn right side out and thread narrow ribbon through the holes in the lace near the top.

Fill the bottom of the cone with cotton, to give it body.

Pull the ends of the ribbon together and tie in a bow. A hook may be attached to the lace to serve as a hanger.

SOURCE: *Godey's Lady's Book*, December 1874.

Miss Roly-Poly Yarn Doll

Materials needed:
Ball of white darning cotton
Cardboard eight inches long
Narrow ribbon
Embroidery floss for features

Tools needed:
Scissors
Needle

A ball of white darning cotton is wound over and over a strong piece of cardboard eight inches long. When all of the ball is used up, a thick skein is formed. One end is cut through; then tie a narrow ribbon about halfway.

This is the top of the doll's head. Separate one half the strands into three parts and make a braid. Tie the end.

Tie another strip of ribbon an inch below the first, for the neck. Separate about ten strands on either side of the neck for the arms. Tie these with ribbon about two-and-a-half inches from the neck; then cut off a little beyond the ribbon tie. All the other strands are caught with another ribbon tied about two inches down from the neck, making a waist. The rest of the yarn is the skirt.

A face is embroidered on.

Miss Roly-Poly's chief attraction is that she has no nerves, and although she has no backbone, either, she has a strong constitution.

Source: *Harper's Young People*, 13 December 1892, p. 135.

Crocheted Snowflake

Materials needed:

#20 mercerized cotton crochet thread
Corkboard or heavy cardboard
White paper
Starch
Straight pins (rust-proof)

Tools needed:

Size 11 crochet hook

Ch. 10, sl. st. in 1st ch. to form a ring.

Rnd. 1—Ch. 3, make 17 dc. in ring, sl. st. to top of ch. 3.

Rnd. 2—Ch. 1, 1 sc. in 1st dc., 1 sl. st. in same place as sc. *Ch. 12, 1 sc. in 7th ch. from hook. (This makes a picot.) Ch. 5, *skip* 2 dc.; 1 sc. in *next* dc. Repeat from * all around, and end the last repeat with sl. st. in first sc. (6 picots).

Rnd. 3—S1. st. along the ch. 5. *In the first picot space, work (2 sc., 3 ch.) 7 times, and 2 more sc., ch. 6, repeat from * all around, and end with sl. st. in first sc. Fasten off.

To make a hanger, attach the thread to the top of the fourth picot of any group and make a chain of the length desired. S1. st. to first ch. and fasten off.

Cover a piece of corkboard or heavy cardboard with clean white paper.

Dip the snowflake in strong starch, spread to shape on the paper, and pin out all the points evenly. Allow it to dry thoroughly before removing the pins.

Godey's Lady's Magazine for December 1866 featured a pattern for a similar crochet design.

Note: A larger crochet hook will give a larger snowflake with a lacier look.

Source: Design by Vi Simms, in *Christmas Decorations from Williamsburg's Folk Art Collection* (Williamsburg, Va.: Colonial Williamsburg Foundation, Publishers, 1976), p. 49. (Distributed by Holt, Rinehart and Winston.)

Christmas Cookies

1 cup butter or margarine	3 cups flour
½ cup sugar	1 teaspoon baking powder
1 egg	¼ teaspoon salt
1½ teaspoons vanilla	½ teaspoon lemon juice

Beat together the first four ingredients until creamy. Add dry ingredients and lemon juice; then chill for several hours. Roll out; use a stockinet sleeve for rolling pin and a pastry cloth so the dough won't stick. Cut in shapes. Bake at 375° F. for eight to ten minutes. When cool, decorate with colored frosting.

Source: *American Agriculturist,* December 1894, p. 469.

Gingerbread Men

Gingerbread men were very popular, and often a Santa Claus seal was pasted on for the face, after baking. The gingerbread men were also painted gold, as were small apples and nuts. If there are a number of items to be painted, the easiest method is to place the objects on waxed paper and use a gold spray paint out of doors.

This is my favorite gingerbread-boy recipe:

¾ cup shortening	2⅓ cups flour
1 cup sugar	2 teaspoons soda
1 egg	1 teaspoon cinnamon
½ cup less 1 tablespoon molasses	1 teaspoon ginger
	1 teaspoon cloves

Mix first four ingredients; mix dry ingredients, add slowly to first mixture. Chill dough. Roll and cut into shapes. Bake at 375° F. for fifteen minutes. Cool and decorate.

Homemade Clay for Tree Ornaments
(Not Edible)

Materials needed:
1 cup corn starch
2 cups baking soda
1½ cups cold water
String
Paint
Clear shellac

Tools needed:
Saucepan
Plate
Damp cloth
Knife or cooky cutter
Brush

In addition to the cookies mentioned, the ladies of the past century made cookies that were very hard and were used just for tree ornaments. Today we can get the same effect by making cookies that look good enough to eat, but aren't, by using clay instead of dough.

In saucepan, stir thoroughly 1 cup corn starch and 2 cups baking soda; mix in 1½ cups cold water. Heat, stirring constantly, until mixture reaches a slightly moist, mashed-potato consistency. Turn out on a plate and cover with a damp cloth. When the clay is cool enough to handle, knead it like dough.

To shape clay, roll out to quarter-inch or half-inch thickness and cut with a knife or cooky cutter. Decorations made of this homemade clay may be cut into animal shapes, hearts, and stars. (See "Sources.") Pierce a hole near the top for string. Let dry; then paint with tempera, gouache, or water colors. When that dries, brush on a final coat of clear shellac to protect the surface.

Cooky Ornaments
(Edible and Inedible)

Cookies were used as tree decorations in all levels of Victorian society. Almost every ethnic group has its favorites. The Pennsylvania Dutch also hung pretzels on their trees. Many cookies were made by pressing dough into wooden molds, then baking. These molds are not easy to find, but occasionally at crafts shows one sees new molds similar to the old ones. Many familiar shapes may be made by using available cooky cutters or tracing around a cardboard pattern. Butter cookies rolled a little thicker than usual with a hole poked in the top for a hanger before baking will look like the old-fashioned kind.

These cookies may be decorated with colored frostings.

Prune-Man Chimney Sweep

Materials needed:
Prunes
Wire (21-gauge)
Small sticks
Paper (white)
Glue
Ink
Net bag
Thread

Tools needed:
Wire cutters
Pen
Scissors
Needle-nosed pliers

The prune-man chimney sweep is made by wiring prunes together to achieve the result shown in the finished sketch. The wire was doubled over so that there would be a loop at the ends of the arms and feet to hold the prunes securely.

Wire each part of the body separately; then join the wires at the trunk, twisting the ends with needle-nosed pliers and pushing them back into the prune and out of sight.

Use two prunes for the body, two for each arm, with one going vertically for the hand; two for each leg, with one going horizontally for each foot. Wire a small bundle of sticks together for the broom.

Cut a small piece of paper into the form of a triangle, glue it together to form a cone, and glue to head. Cut an oval piece of paper for the face, drawing the features with black ink before gluing it in place.

The net bag is made from a large vegetable bag cut down. Tie the top and bottom of the net with thread.

SOURCE: Adelia Beard and Lina Beard, *What a Girl Can Make and Do* (New York: Scribner's, 1902), p. 244.

Little Girl Egg

Materials needed:
Egg
Red felt
Paper girl face
Glue

Tools needed:
Large needle or
   small pick
Scissors

With a large needle or small ice pick, make a hole about the size of a dime in the small end of the egg and shake out the contents. This is much easier than poking a hole in each end and blowing out the egg. Since the bottom of the egg will show, it is much better not to have a hole in it. Rinse out the inside of the egg and allow it to dry.

Cut two pieces of red felt, shaped like the above outline, 2¼ inches tall, 3½ inches wide, with a 1½-inch head. Glue the face of a little girl on one side. Faces may be found on Christmas cards, wrapping paper, or seals.

Glue the outer edges of the felt head together, then glue the bottom curve to the egg. Cut two round circles for buttons. A felt bow may be added, under her chin, and another piece cut and glued to the back of the head for a hanger.

SOURCE: Harriet Beecher Stowe Collection, Hartford, Connecticut.

More Egg Fancies

Nests

Materials needed:
Eggshells,
Glue (Elmer's, Sobo)
Dried sheet moss
Cotton
Candy eggs

Tools needed:
Small scissors

Birds' nests look very attractive in the tree. Take some halves of eggshells and trim off any rough edges. Paint them inside and out with two coats of white glue to strengthen them. While the second coat is wet, glue sheet moss to the outside of the shell. Line the inside with cotton and add candy eggs.

SOURCE: Caroline L. Smith, *American Home Book of Indoor Games* (Boston: Lee Shepard Pub., 1874).

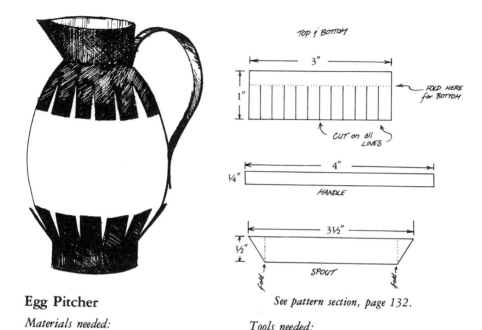

TOP & BOTTOM

3"

1"

FOLD HERE
for BOTTOM

CUT on all
LINES

¼"

4"

HANDLE

3½"

½"

fold

SPOUT

fold

Egg Pitcher

See pattern section, page 132.

Materials needed:
Eggshell
Colored construction paper
Gold foil paper
Glue

Tools needed:
Small sharp scissors
Brush

With the points of the scissors make a hole the size of a dime and shake out the egg. Rinse and let dry. Paint the egg with two coats of glue to give it strength. To turn the egg into a pitcher, cut out gold or colored paper according to the sketches. Cut on the lines and glue the fringed paper to the egg; the uncut portion forms the base. The top is done the same way, with the addition of a spout. Glue the handle to the spout and the egg.

SOURCE: Smith, *American Home Book of Indoor Games.*

Assorted Ornaments

Baskets made of moss and filled with natural flowers added fresh beauty to a tree. Glue sheet moss to the outside of small purchased baskets; line them with foil; add a small piece of Oasis or sphagnum moss and insert fresh flowers into that.[10]

Balls of cake, frosted all over, were thought to look like snow balls.

Pine cones may be spray-painted silver or gold.[11]

Popcorn was mentioned earlier as a good material for making garlands.

Popcorn balls were also hung on the tree—tied with ribbon or string; they should not be wrapped in plastic paper.

If you hang candy canes on the tree and you want it to be truly Victorian, remove the paper wrapping.

Candies of all kinds were put in cornucopias, baskets, boxes, or trays, and eaten when the tree was dismantled on Twelfth Night.

"Sugar plums" were candies, but candied fruits were also hung on the tree.

One account of a Victorian tree mentions silvered pea pods—more than likely, they were catalpa tree pods, which look wonderful painted silver, and so do chestnuts.

Small apples may be gilded or painted with glue and rolled in "diamond dust," our substitute for the ground mica of yesterday.

Nuts were painted silver or gold. If you don't care to paint them, roll them in silver or gold foil, with two or three strung together for greater decorative impact.[12]

The Living Christmas Tree

Materials needed:
Lightweight cardboard
Green felt (approx. 8 yards)
Cape pattern size 12 to 14
  (Butterick 3361)
Green thread
Poster board (lightweight cardboard)
Hula hoop
Straight pins
Glue

Dowel
Gold foil paper
Velcro
Assorted Victorian-type
  tree ornaments
Fine wire or hooks
Small bells
Tools needed:
Scissors
Needle

Why not make a few more ornaments than you need, especially light-weight ones, and use them to decorate a "Living Christmas Tree?" This is not a live evergreen, but a costume for a young girl—see color section, Plates 8 and 9.

The original had as its foundation a cloak made of green cambric, with green tissue-paper fringe for a leafy effect. In the modern version, green felt is used for the cape and the fringe. Felt was chosen because it is strong, doesn't ravel, hangs well, and may be glued as well as stitched. The pattern to be used for the cape is Butterick 3361, without a hood. Approximately

Instead of live evergreens, this intriguing bit of holiday flamboyance emphasizes a real, live girl—dressed as a Christmas tree. Her hat (left) is a triangle of felt-covered posterboard; her cloak is green felt.

eight yards of felt is needed for the cape, hat, and fringe, using the medium-sized pattern for sizes 12 to 14.

Make the cape according to the pattern directions. Instead of turning up the hem in a normal manner, pin it over a Hula-Hoop, then stitch it by hand. The hoop makes the hem stand out in a circle. Sew small bells around the bottom of the hem, so that the cape will make a tinkling noise as the young lady steps about the room.

Sew hooks and eyes on the front closing.

The hat is made of poster board covered with felt. Cut the cardboard in a triangle, with the longest side the same as the model's head measurement plus one inch for the overlap, and eighteen inches for the height. Roll the triangle to a cone shape and glue. Cut a piece of felt the same size and glue over the cardboard frame. Sobo glue is good, since it doesn't stain the fabric. Place the hat on the model's head and measure the distance from the bottom of the hat to the shoulders of the cape. Cut a strip of felt to that measurement. Pin or glue that piece of felt to the bottom of the hat and then to the shoulders, making a smooth line from the top of the hat to the bottom of the cape.

Before proceeding any further, cut a small hole in the top of the hat and insert a dowel to which a gold paper star has been attached.

The cape is ready for its leaves of fringe. Cut strips of felt five inches wide, fold them over and cut through the folded side leaving an uncut heading which will be stitched to the cape. Beginning at the bottom, sew the fringe around the cape, allowing it to reach to the edge of the hem. Above the first row of fringe, and overlapping it, sew the second row. In this way, put on row after row of fringe, always overlapping it until the cape is covered; then continue the fringe all the way to the peak of the hat. It seems easier to do this stitching by hand, using large basting stitches, than to do it by machine. You stop, of course, at the front opening, so that the young lady may be helped into and out of the cape.

When all the fringe has been attached, it's time to decorate the costume. Start with the garlands, such as popcorn, paper chains, or tinsel. Stitch or pin the garlands in loops.

Decorate the tree in the Victorian manner, using light-weight ornaments.

Allow garlands and tinsel to hang free along the cape opening until the "Christmas Angel" is helped into the cape; then they may be pinned into place.

Since the model would soon tire of standing still, while the cape is being decorated, hang the cape on a hanger or some sort of similar contrivance while decorating it.

This can be made for a party, Christmas Eve, Christmas Night, or a school pageant. It will surely cause a sensation whenever it is worn!

Source: Lina Beard and Adelia Beard, *Things Worth Doing and How to Do Them* (New York: Scribner's, 1906), pp. 174-177.

The Bonbon Man

Materials needed:

1½-inch styrofoam ball
Nylon stocking
Wire (21-gauge)
Wire (27-gauge)
Styrofoam cone (9 inches tall)
Cotton batting
Masking tape
Pins
Red felt
Glue (Sobo)
Black felt
Gold foil wrapping paper
Red satin
Red thread
Red satin ribbon
Small gumdrops
Miniature artificial
   Christmas tree
Tiny baby-doll

Tools needed:

Sharp knife
Scissors
Needle-nosed pliers
Needle

Framework for the Bonbon Man of the 1800s.

Another doll-type decoration is the "Bonbon Man." The original decorations start out by saying, "Procure a wooden doll about eighteen inches in height, break off the arms, substitute wires . . ." It's hard to imagine any of us doing that, so let's make a few substitutions.

Stretch a square of brown nylon stocking over a 1½-inch styrofoam ball, holding the stocking in place with a 6-inch length of wire—this will be the head. Needle-nosed pliers come in handy for twisting wire firmly. Do not cut off the wire; instead, put it aside while the main body is made ready.

Using a sharp knife, round off the styrofoam cone, as shown in the sketch, for the trunk of the doll. Insert a 21-gauge wire twelve inches long through the top of the cone for the arms and another wire the same size and length at the bottom of the cone, for the legs. Wrap the arms and legs with strips of cotton batting to fatten them up and then cover them with nylon

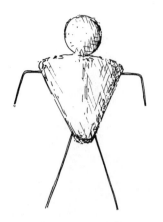

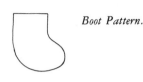

Boot Pattern.

Today's Bonbon Man begins with head and body cut from styrofoam, with light wire arms and legs. (See pattern section, page 136.)

stockings. Tape or pin to cone to hold them in place. Cut four red felt mittens—exact-size patterns for mittens and boots on pages 136–137. Glue the mittens to each arm, with the wire between each piece. Proceed the same way when cutting and applying the boots. Cut pieces of black felt for eyes and eyebrows and red felt for the mouth. Glue into place.

Insert the twisted wires from the head into the widest part of the cone (representing the shoulders).

Cut two strips of gold paper 1½ inches wide and 18 inches long; turn ¼ of an inch over, the length of the paper, and fringe the opposite side ¾ of an inch. Start at the bottom and wrap fringe around each leg; secure to the body with tape or a pin.

Cut two strips 1½ inches wide and 12 inches long; treat the same way and wrap arms from wrist to elbow.

Cut more strips for hair fringe, one row in front and two around the back. Make a cornucopia hat 6½ inches by 9 inches. Glue it to the head, bending down the tip; attach a gold star to the end.

The tunic is made of red satin, or any bright silk. Cut a pattern from the measurements on page 137. Stitch sides and underarms; glue gold paper fringe to bottom of tunic and sleeves. Two strips of fringe 20 inches long will be enough for the tunic and hair.

Cut a circle 5 inches in diameter; cut a circle for the head and cut down the back. Put in place; glue back.

Tie a satin ribbon around the waist for a sash; tie gold-painted hemlock cones to the sash all the way around.

For the Bonbon Man to live up to his name, he must now be covered with bonbons. Small gumdrops seem best for this purpose. They can be either wired or stitched to the body but should be attached to the legs, hanging

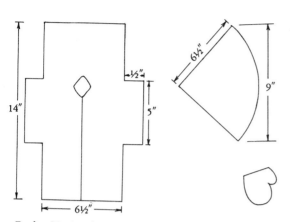

Bonbon Man's red satin tunic is cut as shown at left. Add red felt mittens, boots, cornucopia hat, and gumdrops to his costume and this dapper fellow matches his Victorian forebear. (See pattern section, page 137.)

down in a row under the tunic, over the tunic, under the collar, and on the sleeves. A small Christmas tree is to be placed in one arm and a tiny doll in the other.

SOURCE: *Godey's Lady's Book*, December 1880, p. 576.

Treetop Angel

Materials needed:

Plastic bottle, 7 inches high
  (preferably waisted)
Ping-Pong ball, wooden bead,
  or china doll's head
Yellow thread or yarn
Yellow acrylic paint
Gold or silver foil wrapping paper
Gold or silver ½-inch trim
Glue (Elmer's or Sobo)
Felt-tipped pen
Masking tape
Silver or gold thread
Lipstick

Tools needed:

Scissors
Paint brush
Sharp knife

65

An angel usually hovered over the treetop, and the Nuremberg Angel made with a china head and tinfoil body was typical of the period.

To make an angel of your own, decide first whether you want to attach it with a hanger to the topmost branch or have it stand up on top. If you want it to go on top of the branch, rather than to be tied to it, cut a circle in the bottom of the plastic bottle mentioned under materials; this will enable you to slip the finished angel over the top of the branch.

Then glue a wooden macrame bead to the top of the plastic bottle—or use a Ping-Pong ball for the angel's head. Draw the features, using a felt-tipped pen; use lipstick or water colors for the lips and rosy cheeks. If you have a doll's head of wood or china, in the proper size, use that, of course.

To make a 9-inch angel, use a bottle 7½ inches tall, including the neck. Wind yellow yarn around the doll's head. Glue it, here and there, so that it will stay in place. Tie a string in either silver or gold thread around the angel's neck, with a loop toward the back for attaching to the tree.

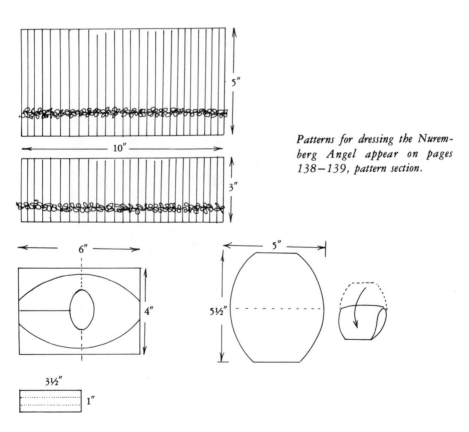

Patterns for dressing the Nuremberg Angel appear on pages 138–139, pattern section.

Any gold or silver foil or wrapping paper will do for the dress and wings. For the underskirt, accordian-pleat paper 5 inches by 10 inches. A strip of metallic ribbon may be glued to the paper before pleating. The overskirt is 3 inches by 10 inches, made the same way. After the underskirt is pleated, overlap one end over the other and glue in place, forming a skirt. Overlap at the waist here and there and tape in place. Treat the overskirt the same way. Don't worry about the tape; it will be covered by the bodice.

For the bodice, cut a piece of paper 6 inches by 4 inches; make a circle in the middle for the head and cut from the circle to one end, as shown in the sketch, page 138; this is the back. Glue metallic trim to the bodice; fit to the angel, gluing the back by overlapping slightly; then glue each side, giving her a nipped-in waist.

Cut four wings 5½ inches by 5 inches; glue wrong sides together, then bend—but do not crease—each wing, gluing the curved edges in place behind the angel.

SOURCE: Phillip V. Snyder, *The Christmas Tree Book* (New York: Viking Press, 1976), p. 60.

2"

5"

A pleated paper skirt is taped to the plastic-bottle body (left). The head can be a wooden bead or a Ping-Pong ball. Metallic trim glued to a paper bodice completes the costume (right). Wings are of foil.

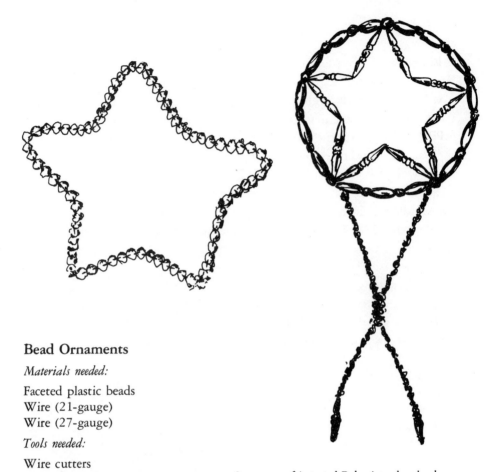

Bead Ornaments

Materials needed:

Faceted plastic beads
Wire (21-gauge)
Wire (27-gauge)

Tools needed:

Wire cutters
Needle-nosed pliers

Ornaments of imported Bohemian glass beads.

These ornaments are copies of Bohemian glass ornaments that were imported in the late 1880s.

The plastic beads recommended here are the exception to the visible-plastic theory, since they resemble the glass beads, except in price.

Cut an 18-inch length of 21-gauge wire; bend one end over a half-inch. String the beads onto the wire, allowing enough wire at the end to join with the other end by twisting the wire ends together. Form into stars, circles, hearts. Extend the length of the wire to form stars inside of circles. Hold them in place with fine 27-gauge spool wire.

The Victorians liked their trees to sparkle with color, glitter, and frost, or its equivalent. These ornaments helped them achieve their goal.

Source: Snyder, *The Christmas Tree Book*, p. 77.

Old Father Christmas

Materials needed:
Five fir cones
Wire (21-gauge)
Apple
Lemon juice
Blue beads (map tacks)
Red felt
Melted paraffin (optional)
Dried sheet moss (optional)
Glue (Sobo)
Purchased artificial tree
Net vegetable bag
Blue construction paper
Small candies
Stems
Cotton (or polyester fiber)
Craft pipe cleaners

Tools needed:
Wire cutters
Sharp knife

The original Old Father Christmas was made to stand on a table or hang on a tree. The reproduction is less ambitious and will only hang on the tree.

Directions for making the original can be described as sketchy, at best, giving only descriptions, not directions, for this interesting ornament.

The body for the original was composed of five fir cones and ours has five pine cones; but the original head and hands were made of papier-mache and the boots were carved of wood. Since exact reproduction of those features would make this project very time-consuming, we have made the following substitutions:

Five pine cones are each wired near the top and then wired together to form the body. The hands and feet are made of double pieces of black felt glued together and then glued to the pine cones.

To make the head, carve an apple face, which is very easy to do: just peel and core the apple; then make indentations for the eyes and mouth and cut a little away for the cheeks. To keep the apple from turning brown, rub a little lemon juice into it. Place it on a tin in a 150-degree oven for twenty-four hours, or until dry, not cooked. Drying time may take longer, depending upon the apple, the temperature, and so on.

Father Christmas's dried-apple head is tied to the pine-cone body with two pipe cleaners. The look is the same, but today's Old Father Christmas has a dried-apple face instead of papier-mache; a pine-cone instead of a fir-cone body; felt instead of wooden boots; and a beard of polyester fiber.

After the apple face is thoroughly dry, dip it in melted paraffin, to give it a porcelain effect. Insert blue beads for eyes—map pins purchased from a stationery store were used here. Glue on cotton or polyester fiber for eyebrows, hair, and beard, and make a circle of red felt for the hat.

The head is attached to the body, as shown in the sketch, with two chenilles (craft pipe cleaners) twisted through the head and then around the pine cone. Glue the hat in place.

If necessary, glue a waistband of dried sheet moss in place to cover wires.

The four-inch Christmas tree is a purchased one, decorated with tiny odds and ends, and glued to the mitten. The "basket of blue cardboard" in original versions is a cornucopia made of blue construction paper filled with small candies; the "net" is a small mesh bag made from a larger vegetable bag.

A bundle of stems (representing switches) is glued to the other red mitten—for the bad boys and girls!

We have no measurements for the original doll, but the reproduction is eleven inches tall.

Source: *Godey's Lady's Book*, December 1868, p. 536.

The Color Plates

Plate 1. "Kissing balls" of evergreens and mistletoe hang overhead at the Christian Heurich Mansion in Washington, D.C. Yuletide tradition is that anyone passing under the mistletoe is likely to be kissed. Custom dates from the time of the Druids, who held mistletoe sacred.

Plate 2. The American Victorian Christmas Tree, prepared yearly since 1976 for the "Trees of Christmas Exhibit" by the Smithsonian Institution's Office of Horticulture. Research, design, and decoration for the tree are by Author Sunny O'Neil.

Plate 3. Ribbon and lace on a cardboard figure add elegance to the Victorian tree in the "Trees of Christmas Exhibit."

Plate 4. A paper fan trimmed with ribbon and bow brightens the Victorian tree in the Smithsonian display.

Plate 5. In red tunic with gold-foil trim, "the Bonbon Man" lounges beside a popcorn garland on the Smithsonian's Victorian tree.

Plate 6. Delicate lace-glove potpourri, found only on such authentically dressed Victorian trees as this one, the Smithsonian's.

Plate 7. Silver ribbon and lacelike doily set off a paper flower at the Smithsonian exhibit.

Plate 8. Strikingly different: the "Living Christmas Tree," a mannequin dressed in a green tree-shaped costume trimmed with miniature ornaments.

Plate 9. Detail of small-scale ornaments decorating the "Living Christmas Tree."

Plate 10. Two cake pans and a broomstick form the foundation for this splendid Christmas table centerpiece at the Christian Heurich Mansion.

Plate 11. Holly centerpiece for this festive Christmas table at the Christian Heurich Mansion rests on a styrofoam base.

Plate 1

Plate 2

Plate 3

Plate 4

Plate 5

Plate 6

Plate 7

Plate 8

Plate 9

Plate 10

Plate 11

Christmas-Tree Ornaments to Buy

Glass ornaments
   (balls,
   reproductions of animals,
   ships, etc.)
Wax ornaments
Colorful Victorian reproductions
   of children's books
Brightly wrapped
   boxes and packages
Reproductions of metal
   candle holders

Small metal baskets
Small flags
Wooden toys
Miniature toys
Dollhouse furniture
Small musical instruments
   made of metal

Avoid any visible plastic—except plastic icicles; they are the only kind of icicles available, now that lead icicles are no longer made. At least they don't have a plastic *look*. Lead icicles were imported from Germany in 1878.

Ornaments were also made of papier mache and metal; these are not being reproduced widely today, but perhaps you may come across them in antique shops.

Toys and gifts both wrapped and unwrapped were hung on the tree. Some ideas and instructions for these may be found in chapter I.

If just half the things described here are put on the Christmas tree, it will become a fairyland.

SOURCE: Snyder, *The Christmas Tree Book*, p. 63.

Christmas plum pudding.

IV Christmas Dinner

Almost all that has been anticipated for Christmas Day has been realized. The presents have all been distributed; the givers and the receivers have exclaimed, praised, and thanked one another and themselves on the taste, ingenuity, and beauty of the gifts. Now everyone is looking forward to a very special dinner. The table has been set with the finest linens and china, and table decorations have been added according to the whim, pocketbook, and talent of the hostess.

In Victorian times, evergreens formed the major part of these decorations, since greens were always available, in the yards and fields of those who lived in the country and in profusion in the markets for the city dwellers. Those who could afford to bought flowers from the florist and mixed them with the Christmas greens; others used cut flowers from their conservatories or window gardens. Forcing bulbs for this purpose was common practice.[1]

Forcing bulbs isn't difficult and is definitely worthwhile. Tulips, hyacinths, and narcissus can be made to bloom in this way, but always read the directions on the container before potting these plants. Buy the bulbs early in the fall. Force a few bulbs at a time and keep the rest under refrigeration. Paper-white narcissus may be planted in gravel, marble chips, or anything that drains easily, in a container three or four inches deep. Place the bulbs, points up, on top of the gravel, then add enough additional gravel to support the bulbs. Add water to cover one half-inch of the base of the bulbs, but don't cover them completely. Put them in a cool, sunny place and keep the water-level stable. If you plant the bulbs around Thanksgiving, they should bloom for Christmas. If they become too tall and have a tendency to fall over, tie them with red ribbon for support—and to make them look even more festive.

Those Victorians who were very foresighted picked the last rosebuds grown in the fall, dipped the ends of the stems in melted paraffin, then wrapped the flowers in tissue paper and placed them in a cool dresser drawer until Christmas Day. Then the roses were recut and placed in warm water, and they bloomed for that one day.[2]

If the family could not afford fresh flowers, the hostess depended upon dried materials, such as sumac, cockscomb, and berries of all kinds for color.

Advice seemed always to be needed—and, one hopes, heeded—in the ladies' magazines. One writer in the 1890s advises her readers not to attempt more than they can easily accomplish, suggesting that a simple decoration well done will be more pleasing than an elaborate one poorly executed. This is especially important in decorating the table, since almost everything is at eye level. More liberties may be taken when decorating the rest of the house.

A great deal of attention was given to the Christmas table because it was thought that, at the very least, an arrangement of greens or a simple bouquet of flowers helped to make the dinner bright and cheerful. When greens were used alone, a bunch of mistletoe was hung from the chandelier, and a basket of holly with its berries was placed in the center of the table. Several sprays of holly and mistletoe, tied with scarlet ribbon, were placed about the table. If other greens were used, bright red sumac was hung from the candelier, with bittersweet massed on the table under it and sprays placed here and there on the cloth.[3]

Sometimes ferns were used alone or combined with lily of the valley, violets, orchids, or roses. Tiny bunches of the same flowers used in the centerpiece were placed, in a carefully casual fashion, here and there on the cloth.

When no flowers were available to add color to a table decorated only with greens, red candles were used to brighten up the arrangement, and a strip of colored cloth was placed down the center of the table. The cloth was either plush or velvet, with sprays of leaves laid along the edges.

The foundations for elaborate centerpieces can be made of simple materials found around the house. For instance, in the drawing on page 87, the container holding the flowers is made of two cake pans with a connecting wooden pole.

Table Decoration

Materials needed:
2 9-inch pans
Green paint
Heavy metal socket
Scotch super-strength glue
    (or any glue that will
    bond metal to metal)
Pipe (2 inches high) to fit
    in socket
Dried sheet moss
Glue, (Sobo, Elmer's)
Large nail
Wooden support
    (such as broom handle)
Fine spool wire
Wet sand
Oasis or Filfast
Flowers—fresh, dried,
    silk
Fresh greens

Tools needed:
Brush
Hammer
Saw

Humble beginnings of what will become an impressive flower centerpiece: one cake pan, turned upside down and firmly attached to the top of a broom-handle; a second cake pan, firmly fixed to the bottom as a base. (See color plate Number 10.)

The table decoration shown here, made of two cake pans held together with a wooden support, is called a "March stand," named for the man who invented it. To make it, paint the outsides of the pans green. Glue the heavy metal sockets in place with strong glue; center one on the inside of the first cake pan, and the other on the underside of the second cake pan. While the glue is drying, cut the wooden support (broom handle) to a length of twenty-two inches. Screw a two-inch pipe into each socket; place the wooden support in each pipe; to make sure the support is secure, pound a large nail in beside it, as shown in the sketch.

Cover the pole with dried sheet moss held in place with fine spool wire wound around it; if there are bare patches here and there, use glue to hold the moss in place.

To make the arrangement, fill the bottom pan with wet sand and insert large ferns into it, all around the edge and drooping over the sides. Cover the sand with sheet moss; then add leaves and flowers at will, using the centerpiece shown in Plate 10 as a guide. Keep the arrangement low.

Before use, all greens and flowers should be well hardened by cutting the stems and placing the stem ends in very warm water; leaving the cuttings in the water until it cools. After that, they may be stored in a cool place until ready to be arranged.

Use floral foam, such as Oasis, instead of sand for the upper pan, to prevent it from being top-heavy. Decorate in the same general way as the lower pan, but have some ferns standing straight up in the center, giving a fountain effect. The rest should curve downward over the side of the pan. Grasses, lily of the valley, and coral bells give a light, airy look to the whole arrangement.

If these flowers are to remain fresh, they will need to have water added; since the arrangement would be awkward to move and pouring water would be risky, I recommend watering with ice cubes. One or two ice cubes added to the arrangement every day should keep it fresh. If the room is especially warm or dry, add more.

Plastic flowers and greens should not be used, but fresh flowers and greens combine very well with silk and dried flowers and help to lower the cost of the total arrangement.

Source: *American Agriculturist*, June 1869, p. 221.

Christmas Table Setting

Materials needed:

Green styrofoam,
   12 inches by 14 inches
   by 2 inches
Holly
Red velvet ribbon (2 inches wide)
10-inch-high styrofoam cone
Dried German statice
Green floral spray
Miniature tree ornaments
Red flowers (roses, etc.)
Red satin ribbon

Mistletoe
11-inch styrofoam bell
Red cockscomb
Velverette glue
   (or any strong, thick craft glue)
Red satin ribbon (1 inch wide)
Red satin fabric
Sobo glue
Red floral spray (optional)
Place cards

Tools needed:

Sharp knife
Clippers
Scissors

The table shown in Plate 11 measures 54 inches by 96 inches, and the decorations are made in proportion to the table. If the table you are decorating is larger or smaller, change the sizes given here to correspond with yours.

The holly centerpiece is 12 inches by 14 inches by 2 inches, and consists of holly leaves and berries pushed into styrofoam measuring that size. Red velvet ribbon is glued around the edge to hide the styrofoam and give the plateau a finished look. Leave a place in the center for the tree.

The tree is made by inserting short pieces of dried German statice into a styrofoam cone 4 inches in diameter and 10 inches high. When the cone is completely covered, spray it with green floral spray, using a green as close in color to the holly leaves as possible. If it is not possible to match the two colors, separate the holly and the tree with a ring of berries or red flowers. This tree may be kept from year to year.

If you prefer a fresh tree, but one that can still be made ahead of time, use long-lasting boxwood. The styrofoam may be used for the base or a block of wet floral foam (Oasis) can be trimmed to a tree shape, with short pieces of boxwood inserted into that.

The tree may be decorated with small, bright presents of perhaps silver thimbles for the girls and ladies, and pencils and whistles for the men and boys. Since Christmas was one of the few days when the children "graced the festive board," they, as well as the grownups, were remembered with these tokens.

At either end of the table are candelabra with red candles. At each lady's place is a corsage of bright red flowers tied with red ribbon; for the gentlemen, there are boutonnieres of mistletoe.

Suspended over the table is a large bell covered with red flowers. The Victorians made their bells of three hoops, in graduated sizes, covered with fabric. The bell used here is styrofoam, eleven inches in diameter and eight inches high, lined with red satin, (any red fabric will do) that has been glued in place with Sobo glue. The outside of the bell is covered with dried cockscomb heads held in place with Velverette glue. Break off small pieces of cockscomb to fill in spaces so that none of the plastic will show. Any red flowers may be used, either fresh or dried, and the lining may be of flowers instead of fabric. If some of the dried flowers have faded or there is too much variation in shades of red, the bell may be sprayed with a red floral spray. The dried-flower bell may be used year after year if stored in mothballs.

Eight one-inch-wide red satin ribbons are attached to the bottom of the bell, reaching to each place, where they are glued to the back of the place card, with a bow of the same material covering the end of the ribbon. The place cards are made by folding unlined three-by-five-inch cards in half. Three cards should be glued lightly, so that they stay together; the added weight is needed to hold the ribbon in place.

SOURCE: *The Ladies' Home Journal*, December 1893, p. 6.

An Epergne from Goblets

The following sketches show how to make an epergne by taking a large platter, round or oval, setting an inverted saucer on it, a glass fruit dish over that, and into this two goblets with their feet firmly bound together with ribbon. Tape the goblets together, first; then cover the tape with ribbon. The lower end is inverted, and the upper one stands upright. If preferred, a tall, slender, glass vase may be used in place of the upper goblet. This forms an extemporary epergne.

To fill the epergne, lay ferns and large leaves around the edge of the platter, slipping the stems under the saucer to keep them in place. Heap the plate with fruit, mingling a few flowers in, for color. Over the edge of the top hang ferns, ivy, or smilax, to trail gracefully down and fill in with grapes, or any other fruit. Fill the upper goblet with water and set in it a bouquet from which droops smilax, or some other graceful green, to conceal

With tape, care, and ingenuity, this elegant epergne can be made of two goblets, a platter, a saucer, and a glass fruit dish. Use greenery to conceal your handiwork.

the glasses. Wet sand may be used to hold the flowers in place and keep them fresh.

When grapes are too expensive or unobtainable, bright red and yellow apples, mixed with bittersweet, holly berries, or cranberries will do very well. The berries may be strung on fine wire and made into little loops, as shown in the sketch on page 26.

Each lady should have a button-hole bouquet, composed of several flowers tastefully arranged, while each gentleman has a button-hole flower, which is simply one flower, such as a rosebud, with a leaf as a background. The stems of the flowers should be covered with damp cotton and wrapped in tinfoil, then wrapped with ribbon.

It is stressed that light, feathery foliage is important. Ferns solve this problem nicely, but consider the leaves of carrots, parsley, and ivy.

The *Ladies Home Journal* of 1888 mixes philosophy with practical housekeeping when they say,

The blithe merry Christmas bells are sounding all over the land, and in every household, it should be the aim of every housewife to gladden and make happy its inmates. It is then a pleasure for every wife and mother to prepare with her own hand, or under her supervision tempting dishes, and favorite sweetmeats for the beloved of the household, not forgetting the special fancy of each one. Surely no other puddings, pies, cakes or candies will be relished as hers, into the compounding of which love is so freely mingled. Then days and weeks devoted to this work is not lost.

SOURCE: *The Ladies' Home Journal*, December 1844, p. 16; December 1888, p. 11.

Most Victorian families had an early breakfast; and although hearty, the meal was usually hurried, so that the children could see the tree and open their presents before going to church.

Dinner in the North was usually served at one o'clock, but dinner was at three in the afternoon in the South, the climax of long planning. Every available chair was crowded about a long table, whose leaves extended as far as possible. Nevertheless, the children were often put at a second, smaller table in the next room. Seldom was there a first course; everything was placed on the table, to be eaten at will—main dishes, sides dishes, seasonings, and preserves.

On this day, grace had a particular solemnity. "Father in heaven, we thank Thee for the bounty that we are about to receive—" At once an attendant or attendants materialized with the turkeys, done to a smooth-skinned, almost polished brown, surrounded by potatoes and stuffed vegetables and filled with a highly caloric dressing—of oysters, chestnuts, or corn-meal mixture. With all the dignity of his rank, the master lifted a sharpened knife and got to work.

With the brown meat or the light (preceded by the usual question about preference) went a dark gravy, pickled mangoes, brandied peaches, and other savory accompaniments. At the end of the table stood one or two hams, dark and inviting; a large roast, cold or warm, and a heaping platter of oysters for those who had not had enough of them at breakfast.

Potatoes in two or three styles, vegetables in butter, vegetables with egg, with a flavoring of ham or bacon or meat—the meal continued for two hours or so, with second helpings or third ones, and heads turned discreetly if a fourth were taken. Toward the end, the hostess slipped away and from the kitchen marched a helper, picked for his strength of arm, who beamed as he presented the piece de resistance, the plum pludding. It had been ignited so that the blue flame played around the heavy ball of promised delight.

Applause, cries from the children, calls of approval—as the fire burned down, sections or spoonfuls went to all the adults and some of the older children. By now, all were surfeited, and the women left the table, taking their young with them. On came decanters of wine and plates of nuts and raisins. For another hour, perhaps, the men would talk, and then heads would begin to nod and one after another would drop out of the conversation. Those who stayed regaled one another with recollections of former years, news of neighbors, crops, and conditions, plans for the year ahead, tales about eccentric relatives who collected old silver or young wives.[4]

A typical Victorian Christmas Day menu, while substantial, would not be difficult to reproduce. The hostess usually prepared for twelve people, but the quantity could stretch to a few more than that.

Christmas Day

Bill of Fare

Boned Turkey	Beets	Lemon Pudding, Baked
Stuffed Ham	Cole Slaw	Cranberry Pie
Stewed Oysters	Fried Celery	Fruit, Nuts
Turnips	Candied Sweet Potatoes	Coffee
Mashed Potatoes	Plum Pudding	

SOURCE: *The Ladies' Home Journal*, December 1890, p. 27.

Boned Turkey

The following old recipe may be used, or a turkey already boned may be purchased from your butcher:

The turkey should be a two-year-old gobbler, fat, tender, and large. Dress it nicely, but be careful not to break the skin, save where it is cut just below the breast for drawing and where it has been trimmed. Lay it on a board and with a very sharp knife split it down the back from the neck to the "parson's nose." Lay it on its side, with the breast towards you, and beginning at the back, scrape the meat from the bone downward, until you come to the wing and thigh. Loosen all the meat from the thigh and wing, scraping the bones clean till you come to the joints of the pinions, and the "drum sticks," or leg bones. Leave these in, by separating the joints. They will help to keep the fowl in shape. Continue the scraping until you have loosened all of the meat down to the extremity of the breastbone. Then turn the turkey on the opposite side and proceed as before, leaving on the "parson's nose." Pass the knife around the edge of the breast-bone and the job is finished. Remove the bone and prepare a filling.

SOURCE: *Ladies' Home Journal*, December 1890, p. 27.

Turkey Filling

To one pound of finely crushed lightbread, add half a pound of fresh butter, half a teaspoon of minced-up celery, a salt spoonful of cayenne pepper, salt and pepper to taste, and one gill (one-fourth of a pint) of sweet cream. Mix with this three pints of fresh oysters, from which the liquor has been drained and every atom of shell removed. Mix well and stuff the turkey, sewing it up carefully. Turn it on its back. Place the legs and pinions in a natural position; skewer them down and truss neatly, tying the legs in position with a strand of white thread.

Rub all over with soft butter, sprinkle with salt and pepper, dredge well with flour, and set it into a baking pan. Put it in the oven, pour into the pan one teacupful each of water and oyster liquor, and add one teacupful (a standard measure will do) of butter. Let it roast slowly until thoroughly done, but not overdone. Baste frequently with the gravy in the pan. When done, remove to a hot dish and pour into the pan a teacupful of oyster liquor, and salt and pepper to taste, and, if not thick enough, cream about a teaspoonful of flour with a little butter; stir it in and let it boil a minute or two. Skim the fat off the gravy. This turkey is delicious served cold.

SOURCE: *Ladies' Home Journal*, December 1890, p. 27.

Stuffed Ham

A home-cured ham, nothing less elegant will do for a Christmas dinner, and it should be two years old. Lay it to soak overnight in a boiler full of cold water. When ready to cook it, cut off the hock neatly just above the joint. Scrape and wash it carefully and trim off all of the outer edges, giving it a pretty shape. Weigh it and allow half an hour for it to start to boil, and a quarter of an hour for every pound. Put it in a boiler, cover with cold water, and boil slowly and steadily until done. Keep a kettle of boiling water on the stove, and as the water around the ham boils away, add more, so that it is always well covered. Turn it over when it has been boiling about half of the time allowed for its cooking. When a fork stuck to the bone comes out readily, it is done. Take it up and peel off the skin. If any more trimming is needed, do it now.

Have a stuffing made of one teacupful of bread crumbs just moistened with fresh milk, six grains of allspice and six cloves pounded fine, a pinch of cayenne pepper, a teaspoonful each of finely rubbed thyme, savory, and marjoram, one large tablespoon of butter, and one raw egg mixed together.

With a sharp-pointed knife, make incisions all over the ham about two inches apart. Turn the knife about to make the incision hold as much as possible, then stuff each place full. Rub the ham all over with the well-beaten yolk of an egg. Sift lightly, over that, fine cracker dust and set in the oven to bake slowly for one hour.

SOURCE: *Ladies' Home Journal*, December 1890, p. 27.

My family does not appreciate the saltiness of country ham, so in experimenting with this recipe, I used a precooked shank-half ham. I doubled the stuffing recipe, made incisions as directed all over the ham, even on the cut side, and then covered the outside with a thin layer of the dressing. It was prepared and baked one hour on the day before it was to be served, and baked one hour before serving. In that way, the spices in the stuffing permeated the ham, especially the cloves. I found this to be an unusual dish, good when served hot and equally good cold.

Stewed Oysters

Before cooking oysters, carefully remove all particles of shell. Put one gallon oysters with their liquor into a granite saucepan, salt and pepper to taste, add three quarters of a pound of very nice butter. Oysters require a quantity of butter if you want them in perfection. Frequently stir them, and when they are thoroughly heated through and begin to cook, stir into them one teacupful of fresh cracker dust, finely pounded. As soon as they are done, which is as soon as they plump out, remove them from the fire. Too much cooking, like too little butter, will ruin the oyster. While cooking, stir often from the bottom of the saucepan, otherwise they will burn.

Source: *Ladies' Home Journal*, December 1890, p. 27.

Recipes are not given for turnips, mashed potatoes, beets, or cole slaw.

Fried Celery

No recipe is given for this dish, but it may be made in one of two ways: by sautéing in butter, or deep-fried, in batter.

For either method, cut the celery in short pieces, to enable it to fit into a saucepan, and cook for ten minutes in boiling water. For braised celery, remove from the water, saute in butter until both sides are golden brown. Add stock to cover, season, and simmer gently until cooked.

Or the celery may be dipped in a thin batter and fried after the preliminary blanching.

Baked Lemon Pudding

5 eggs	Grated rind of one lemon
1⅓ cups white corn syrup	½ cup butter, melted
¾ cup sugar	Unbaked 9- or 10-inch pie shell
⅓ cup lemon juice	

Beat eggs well. Add corn syrup, sugar, lemon juice, and grated lemon rind. Add melted butter; beat to mix well. Pour into unbaked pie shell. Bake at 375 degrees for ten minutes; then reduce heat to 350 degrees and bake 25 to 35 minutes longer.

Cranberry Pie

3 cups fresh cranberries	1¼ cups sugar
1 cup raisins	½ cup water
2 tablespoons flour	1 teaspoon vanilla

Prepare pastry and line a 9-inch pie pan. Save remaining pastry for the top. Refrigerate both while you make the filling. Chop cranberries coarsely. Combine with raisins and all remaining ingredients. Place in chilled pie shell, cover with top crust (slashed in several places) and crimp edges together securely. Bake in a preheated 450-degree oven for 10 minutes. Then reduce oven temperature to 350 degrees and continue baking a half-hour longer. Cool before serving.

SOURCE: Ruth Cole Kainen, *America's Christmas Heritage* (New York: Funk and Wagnall's Publishing Co., 1969), p. 47.

Christmas Plum Pudding

1 cup ground suet	1 beaten egg
1 cup raisins	½ teaspoon soda
2 cups dry bread crumbs	1 teaspoon cinnamon
½ cup chopped nuts	½ teaspoon cloves
1 cup sugar	½ teaspoon allspice
½ cup milk	½ teaspoon salt

Mix all ingredients well and pour the batter into a greased pudding mold. Cover. A tin can may be substituted, if filled two-thirds full and properly greased. Cover with a lid or with foil held securely in place.

Steam for two hours in boiling water. Be sure the water is kept boiling. Unmold and serve hot with a sprig of holly in the center.

Oatlands Mansion, on Route 15, six miles south of Leesburg, Virginia, is a property of the National Trust for Historic Preservation. The house is decorated for Christmas (and open to the public) in November. Mrs. Grayson Carter Beach, who was born at Oatlands, described her 1867 Christmas dinner in this way:

Dinner was in the middle of the day and the Rose Canton China was brought forth: the same centerpiece of holly and flowers from the greenhouse that had been used at breakfast was placed in the middle of that beautiful table and glass bowls of pickles and jellies were added. Turkey and all the trimmings in front of Father; four vegetables in front of Mother—the ham and a tureen of creamed oysters on the sideboard and Alfred, Milly, and Liza waited on the table and saw that everything was as it should be—next came Plum Pudding, two kinds of fruit cake, and also sponge cake. Father sliced the black fruit cake. After the table was cleared, the tall glasses of wine jelly (made from Pig's feet) was brought in. This was served with pitchers of that rich yellow cream. The coffee we had after dinner, and not until the late afternoon did we have the egg nog.

We children were so tired by then that we had only bonnie clabber or junket—we called it *slip*, because it just slipped down. We then went to bed. All the servants were off on Christmas night and the family gathered around the fire in the parlor for evening prayers. Later, all the grownups on their way to bed stopped by the large press in the back hall for another little sliver of turkey or Virginia ham. So ended another Christmas day at Oatlands.[5]

Twelfth Night party-goers await the crowning of the Twelfth Night queen, a high point in the festivities marking the end of the Christmas season on January 5.

V Parties

Home Parties for Young Children

Victorian Christmas parties were held during the twelve days between Christmas Day and Epiphany, January 6, or "Little Christmas."

During the 1800s, parties for special age groups grew popular, especially those geared to children of similar ages instead of groups of children of all ages. Food and games for a group the same age could be planned more easily than for a gathering whose ages varied, and the party itself was more successful, since younger children were not always losing out to older ones.[1]

The general practice was to send out the party invitations in the name of the child being honored, with the party hours usually being between three o'clock and six.

The party supper played an important role in the festivities, and an 1897 *Ladies' Home Journal* gave this advice about the menu:

From the following list of dishes, which are available for children's suppers, menus which are attractive and hygienic may be readily compiled: bouillon, hot and cold; oyster stew, creamed chicken, cold chicken, chicken croquettes, rice croquettes, finger rolls, thin slices of bread and butter, chicken sandwiches; chocolate and vanilla ice cream, lemon and orange ice, orange and lemon jelly, Charlotte Russe, sugar cookies, ladyfingers, sponge cake, cupcakes, and small chocolate cakes.[2]

The soups were served in small bouillon cups with an accompaniment of crackers. Creamed chicken was served in fancy paper patty cases. Bread sliced very thin, then buttered, was cut into intricate forms. Ice cream was especially welcome when it was served in individual forms. Homemade desserts, such as blancmange and jelly, were also most attractive when made in little individual forms. Cakes were small and generously iced. Hot chocolate was the favorite drink, especially when served in after-dinner coffee cups.

Next after the supper in importance—but before it, in point of time—came the entertainment. If any special event had been prearranged, the invitations would announce it, by writing "Spider Web," "Punch and Judy," "Soap-Bubble," or "Fish-Pond," in the lower left-hand corner of the invitation.[3]

To reproduce these parties is not difficult, but for a "Spider-Web Party," elaborate preparations are needed, as noted in chapter I. For a "Punch and Judy" marionette show, professional entertainers were provided.

The old standard games were played at children's parties, as well—games such as "Here We Go 'Round the Mulberry Bush," "Drop the Handkerchief," and "Who's Got the Button."

Procedures and materials for various kinds of parties and party activities follow.

Soap-Bubble Party

Materials needed:

Long, narrow table	Castile soap and water
Blanket (optional)	Glycerine
Sheet (optional)	Prizes
Small basins	Plastic sheeting
Clay pipes	

The long, narrow table was covered with a folded blanket and then with a sheet. Plastic sheeting could be substituted today.

As many small basins and clay pipes as there were children present should be supplied. It's also a good idea to keep some extra bubble-pipes on hand. The suds for bubble-blowing may be prepared the day before the party, with Castile soap (see "Sources"). If a little glycerine is added to the suds, the bubbles will be shinier and stronger. Keep the mixture in a jar until it is ready to be used.

Prizes may be awarded for the longest, shortest, and the greatest number of bubbles at one blow.

A Fish-Pond

Materials needed:

Large tub or clothes-basket	Fishing rods
	String
Small prizes	

A fish-pond is a large tub or a clothes-basket in which various small, wrapped packages are placed. Each package is tied with string, with a loop at the top instead of a bow. A fishing rod with a good-sized hook is provided for each child, and each child is given a certain number of opportunities to capture the gifts.

An Auction Sale

Materials needed:
Small basket or bag

Fifty dried beans
Assortment of prizes

An Auction Sale offers great fun for participants. Each child is provided with a small basket or bag containing fifty dried beans. A large basket containing packages of every shape and size is brought in, and an older person is selected as the auctioneer. These packages may contain things of value or not, but in every case their identity must be hidden by their wrappings. The auctioneer, who has no knowledge of the contents of the parcels, must proceed to describe with great imagination the articles for sale, trying to guess from the shape what the articles may be. The children bid their beans for the prizes, each bean representing one cent, each article being sold at auction to the highest bidder.

A Victorian Christmas Pinata

Materials needed:
Thin white paper
Glue
Assorted prizes
String
Blindfold
Stick

Tools needed:
Scissors

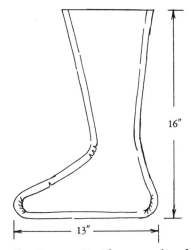

Sock-shaped pattern for making the Victorian pinata.

The Christmas Pinata is a way of distributing small gifts or candies for the younger children and providing a game at the same time.

The pinata can be either a large bag, made of two layers of tissue paper tied with string enclosing the prizes, or a stocking, as shown in the sketch.

To make the stocking, cut out one piece of paper as shown in the drawing, making the foot thirteen inches long and six inches high from the sole to the top of the instep. Make the leg of the stocking sixteen inches long from the heel to the top; then cut another stocking, one inch larger all around than the first. Place the two together; fold the edge of the larger stocking over the smaller piece and paste it down all around except at the top. Fill the stocking with whatever gifts you choose, tie a string around the top to keep it together, and suspend it from the center of the doorway.

Experiment with using two layers of paper; the bag should not rip too easily.

Each child is given a turn at breaking the pinata and releasing the gifts. Each player, in turn, is blindfolded, given a long, light stick, led up within reach of the stocking, and told to strike it. When a player succeeds in striking the stocking and tearing a hole in it, the gifts or candy will scatter all over the floor, to be scrambled for by the players. Each person should be allowed three trials at striking the stocking. An older person should always supervise, since this game could get out of hand.

<small>SOURCE: Adelia Beard and Lina Beard, *What a Girl Can Make and Do* (New York: Scribner's Publishing Company, 1902).</small>

A Peanut Hunt

Materials needed:	*Tools needed:*
Peanuts	Scissors
Rose-colored tissue paper	Toy horn
Light green tissue paper	
Pink or green bag	
Prizes	

For this game, preparations should be made ahead of time by wrapping, separately, a hundred or more peanuts. Wrap most of them in rose-colored paper; wrap a few in light green paper. Hide them all in out-of-the-way places.

When the peanuts have all been hidden, and it's time for the search to begin, give a blast on a toy horn, announcing that the hunt is about to begin. Each player is given a pink or green bag to hold his or her spoils.

The one whose bag is filled first is awarded first prize; the one having the most rose-colored nuts gets second prize, while the one showing the most green ones gets the booby prize.

<small>SOURCE: *American Agriculturist*, November 1896, p. 483.</small>

Parties for Pre-Teens and Teenagers

For pre-teens and teenagers and those a little older, card tricks and magic tricks came high on the list of popularity, with each person taking a turn performing. A white Christmas meant ice-skating and tobogganing parties, with supper at someone's home afterward. Young adults and teenagers were fond of taffy pulls, and in those instances, the candy furnished the game as well as part of the refreshment, along with sandwiches and the favorite drink, hot chocolate. The magazines were full of ideas for party activities; some of them follow.

Eat a Candle

Materials needed:	*Tools needed:*
Apple	Knife
Almond	Match

One of the best party jokes was to pretend to eat a candle. This game should be played in the evening, of course. Cut out a piece of apple, round and as long as your thumb, and shape it so it will look like a candle. In the top of the "pretend" candle, stick an almond, to serve as a wick. Light the wick (the almond); it will burn a full minute and, having thus proved that you are holding a "candle," remove the wick and eat the apple. If cleverly done, this trick will astonish those present.

SOURCE: *Farm Journal*, January 1892, p. 12.

A Candy-Pull

Materials needed:	*Tools needed:*
Many young people	Several sauce pans
Quantities of the supplies listed below	
Aprons	

A candy-pull must be held in the kitchen. Several pans are needed and a good stove, and if the group is very young, two or three grownups must be present to superintend. The superintendents should have on hand a great supply of aprons and good humor.* In 1843, William Bollaert, an English visitor to Texas, described such a party, in which "some fifty lads and lassies congregated to assist. The great fun and sport," he reported, "is to approach

103

slyly the person whose candy appears to be well-pulled and snatch it from them. This produces hilarity."†

SOURCES: *American Agriculturist, March 1882, p. 118.
†Harnett T. Kane, The Southern Christmas Book (New York: David McKay, Inc., 1958), p. 267.

Black-Walnut Taffy

1 cup light corn syrup	2 tablespoons butter
1 cup sugar	1 teaspoon soda
1 cup thin cream	1 cup black walnuts, chopped
1 tablespoon vinegar	

Boil first three ingredients to syrup stage. Add vinegar and continue boiling to the firm-ball stage (254° F). Add butter, soda, and walnuts and pour into a well-buttered platter. Let cool to handling stage; then, with buttered fingers, begin pulling until firm and glossy, ending with a small white rope. Cut into two-inch pieces and wrap in waxed paper.

SOURCE: Ruth Cole Kainen, America's Christmas Heritage (New York: Funk and Wagnall's, 1969), p. 128.

Corn-popping parties also furnished food and fun. The popcorn was served with butter or made into balls by adding molasses or simple syrup.

Party ideas abounded; for instance, a young lady in her mid-teens invited twenty of her girl friends to an afternoon marshmallow-toasting from two to six in the afternoon. The furniture was removed from a large room, and small tables were set with lamps, sticks, and marshmallows. The young ladies played games; ate oyster patties, buttered-bread sandwiches, salad, assorted cakes, and chocolate; and toasted their marshmallows over the lamps.[4]

Games played by young people sitting in a circle included old favorites such as "Gossip," with one person whispering something to the person sitting next to him or her, repeating it to the next person, until the one on the end says the phrase out loud, and, of course, it usually is far removed from the original.[5]

To entertain a group of young people of all ages, a game called "Fling the Towel" was found to be amusing. The party forms a circle, with one person "imprisoned" in the center. Someone in the outer circle then flings a large towel, aiming to hit some other member. If the player in the middle can intercept and catch the towel on its way across the ring, he takes the place of the one who threw it, who then takes his stand in the middle. If the towel hits the person at whom it was aimed, that player must try to get rid of the towel by throwing it to another player before the one stationed in the middle can catch it. [6]

Games played with paper and pencil were considered good ice-breakers. At one social gathering, reported by the *American Agriculturist*, one of the young ladies attending brought an inexpensive autograph album, and each person present took the album, in turn, and drew the picture of a man on an album page. Since they had to draw these pictures with their eyes closed, the results were "highly amusing." Names and dates were added to each effort, and the work became a collection of interesting mementos of the sort so dear to the Victorian heart. [7]

Variations of this idea were often used at parties for all ages. Players were asked to draw pictures of animals (the pig was especially popular), while blindfolded, with prizes for the best and the worst.

"Metamorphosis" is a slightly more sophisticated form of the same game. For "Metamorphosis," each person at the party was furnished a sheet of paper and a pencil. At the top of the sheet, each was to draw the head of a bird, animal, fish, or person, and fold down the sheet so that nothing of the drawing was visible except lines to show on what part of the paper the body should be placed. The first player then passes it on to his next neighbor, who draws on the page a body to suit his own fancy. The page is then folded again and passed to the next player, who must draw legs, two or four. When the papers were completed, some very curious monsters, unknown to natural history, were uncovered. [8]

Parties for Young Adults

A game that many young Victorians enjoyed was called "Literary Salad." The finished product is illustrated below.

Materials needed:

Ink
Green tissue paper
Glue

Tools needed:

Scissors
Pen
Bowl

A bowl of "Literary Salad" —lettuce-green tissue strips on which literary quotations were written. Party-goers took a "helping" and guessed at authors' names.

The host or hostess prepared the "salad" ahead of time by writing a selection of literary quotations on separate slips of paper, each quotation carrying a number. A master sheet listed the number and the author of each quotation. Pieces of grass-green tissue paper were cut and glued to the quotation slips, crumpled to resemble lettuce, and placed in a bowl. Each guest, on being served a "salad," read the quotation aloud and guessed at the author's name. Those making mistakes paid a forfeit.[9]

"Random Descriptions" was another popular pencil-and-paper game. To play it, one of the party, provided with pencil and paper, called on each of the others in turn to name some descriptive adjective, such as *pretty*, *ugly*, *short*, and so on. These words were written in a column on the left. The writer then placed his pencil opposite one of the words and called for the name of one of the party, which was written next to the adjective. The names of the rest of the group were written in order. The writer then started at some other place on the list, and each of the company named a locality, such as "on the house," "under the barn," and so on. When all was completed, the sentences were read aloud. Ludicrous combinations were formed, so that "Sweet Susan" was "before the looking glass, making faces," or "Long John" was "hunting rebels, in the wash-tub."[10]

Games for Older Teenagers and Young Adults

The Trades

(A Game of Pantomime)

Each of the party chooses a trade, which he lists in the following manner:

The shoemaker mends shoes.
The washerwoman washes clothes.
The painter paints a portrait.
The cook kneads bread.
The locksmith hammers upon an anvil.
The spinner turns her wheel, etc.

One of the players acts as king or queen and starts the game by working at his own trade. Meanwhile, all the others must make the movements appropriate to theirs. If the king suddenly changes his trade and takes up that of one of the group, all the rest must remain inactive except the player whom the king is imitating. That player must take up the king's trade, until the king is pleased to adopt another; then that player in his turn takes the king's trade, and all the rest remain idle until the king returns to his original trade, which is the signal for all present to recommence their own. If any of the party makes a mistake, he or she pays a forfeit.

Source: *Fireside Games* (New York: Dick and Fitzgerald, 1859), p. 41.

Poker and Tongs

This is about as noisy a game as can well be imagined. Some small article is to be hidden. The person who is to discover it is sent out of the room while that is being done. Another of the players takes a pair of fire-tongs in one hand and a poker in the other. The seeker of the hidden treasure is called in and begins to hunt for the concealed article. While he is at a distance from the spot where it has been placed, the poker, which is held between the legs of the tongs, is stuck alternately with a slow motion, so as to produce a kind of melancholy music. As he approaches the concealed treasure, the music becomes more lively, and as he recedes from it, more slow and solemn; but when his hand is placed on the spot where the article is to be found, the musician plays a loud and noisy tune on his "uncouth instrument." In cases where the rough music produced by the poker and tongs is offensive, the

107

progress of the player in his search may be announced by assuring him that he is "very cold," "rather warmer," or "burning his fingers," as he approaches or recedes from the hidden object. This game is sometimes called "Magic Music."

Source: *Fireside Games* (New York: Dick and Fitzgerald, 1859), p. 34.

Forfeits

No matter what the game, there had to be a loser, and the loser always had to pay a forfeit. Many of these forfeits were in the form of kissing.

One forfeit was to kiss a candlestick. The loser (if a man) politely requested a lady to hold a candle for him. As soon as she did that, she became a "candlestick," and he kissed her.

Another was to "kiss the one you love the best without being noticed." That forfeit involved kissing all the ladies in the company, one after another, without any distinction.

"The Three Salutes" was a forfeit requiring the loser to "kneel to the prettiest, bow to the wittiest, and kiss the one he loves the best." It was thought the easiest—and most diplomatic—way to get around that one was to kneel to the plainest, bow to the dullest, and kiss the one for whom the forfeit-payer cared the least.

"Kiss your own shadow" was a popular punishment. The culprit not familiar with this forfeit would probably kiss his own shadow on the wall, but realize how foolish that was when he saw some other victim place himself between the light and a lady and kiss his shadow, cleverly focused on her.

More of a game than a forfeit is the following stratagem with cards. Someone takes from a pack of cards four kings and four queens, shuffles them, and without looking at them, distributes them to a proportionate number of ladies and gentlemen. The gentlemen finding himself possessed of the king of hearts kisses the lady holding the queen of hearts, and so on with the rest.[11]

Family Parties

The most commonly given parties in Victorian times were still those given by families for their relatives or other families, including all ages. These festivities centered around food and entertainment, which was usually in the form of dancing, music, impromptu shows, and games.

In large family gatherings with a mixture of ages, the children often planned rather elaborate tableaus bringing to life famous paintings, or performed some simple presentation, equally entertaining, with handkerchief puppets.

Two games were popularly played in a darkened room: "Shadows on the Wall" and "Snapdragon."

In "Shadows on the Wall," shadows of animals and people were made by focusing the shadow-shapes made by two hands with candlelight or lamplight behind them, throwing shadows on the wall, as shown in the sketches below.[12]

"Snapdragon" was played by first placing raisins in a bowl, pouring brandy over them and lighting the brandy. The trick is to pull the raisins out of the bowl without being singed. The burning brandy casts weird lights on the players' faces.[13]

"Magic Lantern" shows were well received, and slides of just about any subject could be purchased.[14]

"Charades" was a game in which all ages could join in—and did, with great enthusiasm. It was played pretty much as it is today, with teams taking turns acting out titles of books, plays, and so on.

Shadows on the wall.

An Informal Evening Party

It was felt that an informal party given with simplicity in a small house could be done with very little trouble and expense, yet could be made very pleasant and enjoyable for the guests.

Invitations were sent out two weeks in advance, in the name of the hostess only, written in the left-hand corner of her visiting card, showing the informality of the occasion.

For an evening party, no matter how simple, the parlor and dining room were to be made as attractive as possible with floral decorations and other pretty devices. The simplicity of the occasion leaves the hostess more leisure to devote to her guests and make their evening more enjoyable.

When dancing was not introduced, pleasant conversation with friends, recitations, or music were all found to be delightful pastimes. An invitation to a guest to sing or play the piano often came from the hostess.

For Victorian ladies attending a small, informal party, quiet evening dress was appropriate. The gentlemen, however, were expected to appear in full dress at all evening entertainments.

Refreshments were dainty and appetizing. The following menu was suggested for those in the country or rural village, although "lighter eatables," such as cakes, fruit, and chocolate were also suitable.[15] These were either served from a side table or the main dining room table. A typical menu for such an occasion follows, with recipes.

Menu for an Evening Party

Broiled Oysters	Lobster Farci
Boned Ham	Chicken Salad
Boned Chicken	Spiced Tongue
Sweetbread Croquettes	Gelatine Pineapple Jelly

Cafe Parfait	Meringues
Banana Ice Cream	Ice Cream Cake
Coconut Cake	Macaroons

Coffee, Tea, Chocolate

Source: *The Ladies' Home Journal*, February 1889, p. 11.

Broiled Oysters

Drain oysters; place them in a buttered pan with butter, salt, and pepper poured over them. Place the pan under the broiler until the oysters are plump. Serve them at once, on toast.

Boned Ham and Chicken

Boned hams and chickens may be purchased from your butcher. They were baked, and served hot or cold.

Sweetbread Croquettes

Soak sweetbreads in cold water for several hours; then drain and cook them slowly in fresh cold water for five minutes after the water starts to boil. Drain again, and let cool. Trim them if the butcher has not already done so.

Chop the sweetbreads, ending up with 2 cups.
Make a cream sauce of:

2 tablespoons butter   1 cup milk
2 tablespoons flour   ¼ teaspoon each salt and pepper

Cook and stir the butter over low heat until it is melted. Slowly add flour until it is a smooth paste, then add milk, stirring with a whisk until the sauce is smooth but not boiling.

Add chopped sweetbreads.
Chill the mixture.

After they are cool, form into the desired shape and roll in 1 slightly beaten egg diluted with 2 tablespoons water, then in 2 cups finely ground cracker crumbs. Place in fry-basket and fry in deep fat until nicely browned. To reheat, place the croquettes in a hot oven for five to ten minutes.

Chicken Salad

2 cups cooked chicken, diced
2 cups chopped celery
4 hard-boiled eggs, chopped fine

Mix and toss lightly with enough French dressing to coat the ingredients.

Add:

1 cup mayonnaise
Salt and pepper to taste

Garnish with celery tops. Served chilled, on a bed of lettuce.

Pineapple Jelly

1 envelope unflavored gelatin	½ cup sugar
½ cup cold water	1½ cups cubed canned pineapple
1 cup hot pineapple juice	(packed in its own juice)

Soften gelatin in cold water, then dissolve in hot juice. Stir in sugar. Set in refrigerator to thicken. Add pineapple. Place in mold and chill.

SOURCE: Fannie Merritt Farmer, *The Boston Cooking School Cookbook* (Boston: Little, Brown Publishing Company, 1947), p. 567.

Cafe Parfait

⅔ cup sugar	2 egg whites
½ cup coffee	2 cups whipping cream
2 egg yolks	1 teaspoon vanilla
	Pinch of salt

Make a strong cup of coffee. Combine sugar and ½ cup of coffee and boil until syrup spins a thread. Pour over well-beaten egg yolks. Beat well. Cool. Fold in well-beaten egg whites. Fold in cream, which has been whipped; add vanilla and salt. Freeze according to your freezer directions.

Banana Ice Cream

6 eggs, slightly beaten	¼ teaspoon salt
2 cups milk	2 cups whipping cream
¾ cup sugar	1½ teaspoons vanilla
2 to 3 tablespoons honey	3 large bananas

In heavy saucepan, mix eggs, milk, sugar, honey, and salt until well blended. Cook over low heat, stirring constantly until mixture thickens and just coats a metal spoon. Cool immediately. Cover with protective wrap; chill thoroughly.

Mash bananas and stir into cooled mixture. When ready to freeze, combine chilled custard with whipping cream and vanilla. Pour into one-gallon ice cream freezer and proceed according to manufacturer's directions.

Coconut Snowball Cake

Coconuts are not native to the South but they have always been plentiful and inexpensive. And, as they began to appear for sale in December, they became synonymous with Christmas holidays. The great Coconut Snowball

Cake which is traditional in many Southern homes is one of the most impressive of creations.

⅔ cup butter, softened	3 teaspoons baking powder
2 cups sugar	½ teaspoon salt
1 cup warm water	8 egg whites, room temperature,
3 cups sifted flour	and beaten stiff
	1 teaspoon orange extract

Grease two 9-inch or 10-inch round cake pans and line with paper on the bottom. Then grease again and dust with flour.

If using electric oven, turn to 350° F to preheat; if using gas oven, turn to lowest heat.

Cream butter and sugar well together, about ten minutes. Begin to add warm water, ¼ cup at a time, alternating with flour to which baking powder and salt have been added. When all water has been added, alternate remaining flour with stiffly beaten egg whites. Add flavoring last.

Divide batter equally between two prepared pans and put in oven to bake. If baking in a gas range, increase heat 25 degrees when they are just well done, not brown or crusted. Turn out on rack.

When cake layers cool, place one upside down on a large, flat platter to be iced.

Icing and Filling

4 cups sugar	4 egg whites, beaten stiff
2 cups hot water or	2 large coconuts, grated
juice of coconut	1 teaspoon orange extract

Place sugar in a saucepan and pour hot water over it. Boil together very rapidly until the mixture forms a soft ball in cold water. Pour a half-cup of hot syrup over stiffly beaten egg whites. Let remaining syrup cook until it spins a long thread or reaches the hard-crack stage when dropped into water. Pour slowly over egg whites, beating constantly. Add flavoring and beat until icing begins to be thick and smooth.

Spread layer of icing one inch thick on cake. Then spread one-inch layer of grated coconut on top of the icing. (Do not mix coconut with icing; it would completely change the character of the cake.) Top coconut with a second one-inch layer of icing. Place second layer on top and cover with a layer of icing one-inch thick. Spread icing down the sides of the cake until cake is white and icing is thick. Sprinkle grated coconut on top, at least one inch thick. Dab coconut around the sides, also, as thickly as it will stick.

If icing will not stand up one inch thick, it is too soft and needs more cooking. In that case, steam it in a double boiler until icing will hold its shape when dropped from a spoon.

Store cake in refrigerator.

SOURCE: Source for both cake and icing from Ruth Cole Kainen, *America's Christmas Heritage* (New York: Funk and Wagnall's, 1969), p. 121. Reprinted by permission of Harper and Row, Publishers.

Tongue in Spicy Aspic

1 smoked beef tongue
Cayenne pepper
½ teaspoon cinnamon
½ teaspoon allspice
½ teaspoon white pepper

¼ teaspoon ground cloves
¼ teaspoon mace
Several sprigs of parsley,
   chopped fine
3 tablespoons vinegar

Cover beef tongue with cold water and cook over a gentle heat for two to three hours, or until very tender when pierced with a fork. Lift tongue from broth. Boil broth over a high heat until it is reduced to about one pint. Meanwhile, skin the tongue and trim the root. Cut the meat in small cubes and season with a dash of cayenne, spices, and parsley. Pack the mixture into a bowl or mold. Mix 3 tablespoons of vinegar into the hot broth, then pour over the meat. Refrigerate overnight. Unmold and cut in slices to serve. Serves eight.

SOURCE: *The American Heritage Cookbook* (New York: American Heritage Publishing Company, Inc., 1964), p. 498.

Ice-Cream Cake
or
The Queen of All Cakes

½ cup sifted cake flour
¼ teaspoon salt
3 eggs, separated
1 teaspoon cider vinegar
½ cup sugar
¼ teaspoon almond extract

Filling:
1 can (3 ½ ounces) blanched
   almonds
¾ cup heavy cream
¼ cup sugar
½ teaspoon vanilla

Grease a jelly-roll pan; line with wax paper and grease the wax paper. Sift flour and salt together and set aside. Beat egg yolks with an electric beater for ten minutes. Wash the blades of the beater, then beat egg whites until

114

frothy. Add vinegar and beat in the half-cup of sugar, a little at a time, until it becomes a satiny mixture that stands in peaks. Stir in almond extract, then fold into yolks gently. Sift flour over the surface and fold in until batter is well blended. Pour into pan and bake in a preheated 350° oven for twelve to fifteen minutes, or until cake begins to pull away from the sides of the pan. *Do not overbake.* Invert on a tea towel sprinkled lightly with confectioners' sugar and carefully pull off wax paper. Beginning with the broad side of the cake, roll it up. Keep towel around the cake to hold its shape, as it cools.

To make the filling: Chop almonds coarsely and toast in a 350° oven until golden. Beat cream until stiff, then stir in sugar, vanilla, and almonds. Unroll the cooled cake, spread the cream filling over the surface, and reroll. Chill before serving, then cut into slices.

This recipe is adapted from *Practical Housekeeping*, where it is called "Ice Cream Cake." The filling is made, the author explains, from thick, sweet cream, beaten "until it looks like ice cream." This elegant deception, the reader is instructed, "is the queen of all cakes."

SOURCE: *The American Heritage Cookbook* (New York: American Heritage Publishing Company, Inc., 1964), p. 591.

Lobster Farci
or
Scalloped Lobster

4 small boiled lobsters (1¼ pounds)	Salt, red pepper, paprika to taste
2 tablespoons butter	½ cup cream
2 tablespoons flour	2 egg yolks
1 cup chicken broth	½ cup sherry wine
	Bread crumbs with butter

Remove meat from cooked lobsters and cut into small pieces. Make a dressing of butter, flour, chicken broth, and seasoning. Simmer a few minutes and then add cream and beaten egg yolks. Stir constantly until thick and smooth. Mix the lobster meat, while hot, in this dressing, then stir in the sherry wine. Put it in the shells previously prepared; fill them up, and put crumbs over them with a little butter. Bake in 400-degree oven until brown.

Makes four servings.

SOURCE: "A Nineteenth-Century Receipt," by Miss Nancy D. Mitchell, in *Maryland's Way*, by Mrs. Lewis R. Andrews and Mrs. J. Reancy Kelly (Baltimore: The Hammond-Harwood House Association, 1963), p. 74.

Meringues

1½ cups sugar	⅛ teaspoon salt
7 egg whites, at	¾ cup sugar
room temperature	1 teaspoon vanilla

Beat egg whites until they are very stiff. Add the sugar very slowly, beating the eggs constantly. When the first batch of sugar has been absorbed, add the rest of the sugar and the vanilla.

Place large spoonfuls of this mixture on a baking sheet covered with a sheet of heavy, brown, unglazed paper that has been moistened. Bake in a very slow oven (225 degrees F.) for about fifty minutes. Remove the meringues from the paper and turn them over, letting the bottoms dry in the turned-off oven, with the door open, for about ten minutes.

If they are to be filled, crush the top with a teaspoon while they are warm. Shortly before serving, fill the hollows with whipped cream flavored with vanilla.

Makes about twelve three-inch meringues.

Macaroons

1 cup sugar	½ teaspoon cornstarch
3 egg whites	½ teaspoon baking powder
½ pound blanched	
ground almonds	

Whip egg whites until stiff; add the sugar slowly, whipping constantly. Fold in the remaining ingredients.

Drop the batter from a teaspoon onto a greased cooky sheet. Bake in a slow oven (275 degrees F.) until they are done, about twenty minutes. Do not allow them to become brown.

Makes about forty macaroons.

A Dainty Christmas Tea

Since the main meal on a Victorian Christmas Day was, generally speaking, rather elaborate, the Christmas tea was made up of light, elegant trifles to contrast with it. The only exception would be the serving of Christmas plum-cake (recipe given in chapter IV).

Guests could be served while seated at the table, or they sat or stood around the room and had the tea and food handed round to them; the choice was up to the hostess.

In any case, the table was made to look as attractive as possible, to stimulate the appetite.

Flowers and ferns should be placed in small finger-glasses or slender vases; or, lacking these, one can arrange holly in long, trailing sprays on a snow-white cloth. Whichever flowers the Victorian hostess chose, she always mixed them with her very best china.[16]

The following recipes have been adapted to today's measurements and ingredients.

Menu

Lemon Patties	Chocolate Macaroons
Fruit Leaves	Curled Wafers
Christmas Plum-Cake	

Lemon Patties
Piecrust

4 cups unsifted all-purpose flour (lightly spooned into cup)	1¾ cups solid vegetable shortening
1 tablespoon sugar	1 tablespoon vinegar
2 teaspoons salt	1 large egg
	½ cup water

Put first three ingredients in large bowl and mix well with table fork. Add shortening and mix with fork until ingredients are crumbly. In small bowl, beat together with fork the half-cup of water, the vinegar, and the egg. Combine the two mixtures, stirring with fork until all ingredients are moistened. Divide dough in five portions and, with hands, shape each portion in a flat, round patty, ready for rolling. Wrap each patty in plastic or waxed paper and chill at least one half-hour.

When ready to roll piecrust, lightly flour both sides of patty; put on lightly floured board or pastry cloth. Cover rolling pin with stockinet and rub in a little flour. Keeping pastry round, roll, from center, to ⅛-inch thickness and 2 inches larger than inverted pan. Fold in halves or quarters; transfer to pie pan; unfold and fit loosely in pie pan. Press with fingers to remove air pockets.

For tart shells: Roll piecrust patty to ⅛-inch thickness as above. Cut in

117

rounds 1 inch larger in diameter than tart pans, rerolling scraps if necessary. Press each round well into tart pan. Even off edges with thumb. Prick bottoms with fork, bake at 450 degrees F. for eight or ten minutes, or until golden brown. Cool.

Makes about 100 tart shells. Keep frozen until ready to use.

Lemon Filling

1½ cups sugar
¼ cup butter

3 eggs
Grated rind and juice
    of 3 lemons

Melt butter and sugar in a heavy pan. Beat eggs in a bowl. Add rind and lemon juice to melted sugar and butter; this should cool the mixture enough for the eggs to be added. Cook, without boiling, until the filling thickens. (Stored in a jar in the refrigerator, this lemon filling will keep a month.)

Fill the baked tart shells with the filling. Serve lightly sprinkled with confectioners' sugar.

Chocolate Macaroons

1 cup purchased almond paste
1 egg white
1¾ cups confectioners' sugar
1 egg white

1 cup confectioners' sugar
¼ cup cocoa powder
1 egg white
¼ teaspoon almond extract

Mix almond paste and one egg white together in blender. Add sugar and second egg white slowly to mixture and blend until smooth. Combine second sugar and cocoa powder and add to mixture. Blend in third egg white and almond extract.

Drop from teaspoon onto cookie sheets covered with thick paper. Bake at 350 degrees F. for eighteen to twenty minutes. Let cool. Remove macaroons from paper by dampening the back of the paper with a wet cloth.

SOURCE: John Zenker and Hazel G. Zenker, *Cookie Cookery* (New York: M. Evans and Company, Inc., 1969), p. 191.

Curled Wafers
(Almond Wafers)

½ cup granulated sugar
½ cup butter or shortening
1 cup all-purpose flour

4 egg whites
1 teaspoon vanilla

Cream sugar and shortening together until light. Sift flour and add to mixture; mix smooth. Beat egg whites until stiff; add vanilla and fold gently into mixture until well incorporated.

Have well-greased or buttered pans ready. Drop 1 teaspoon of batter onto each one. Batter spreads to four- or five-inch circle. Make three on each pan. Bake one pan at a time at 400 degrees F. for ten to twelve minutes, until golden.

Lift up each cookie with a spatula and quickly roll into a cone over the end of a thick wooden spoon handle or a cone-shaped wooden pastry form. Remove cone from handle after it holds its shape; this is about one to two minutes. Let cool. Fill cones with whipped cream just before serving.

Makes ninety or more cones.

SOURCE: John Zenker and Hazel G. Zenker, *Cookie Cookery* (New York: M. Evans and Company, Inc., 1969), p. 191.

Dominoes

½ cup butter	2 teaspoons baking powder
1 cup sugar	⅔ cup milk
2 eggs, beaten separately	1 teaspoon vanilla
1¾ cups flour	Pinch of salt

Cream butter and sugar; stir in lightly beaten egg yolks. Sift flour and baking powder several times and add to mixture alternately with milk. Add vanilla and egg whites, stiffly beaten with the salt. Bake in two 8-inch layer cake pans or one 13-by-9-inch pan at 350 degrees F. for about one half-hour. Cool. Cut with a sharp knife into oblong pieces the shape and size of a domino. Cover the top and sides with white icing; when this has hardened, dip a wooden skewer into melted chocolate and draw, on the iced cookies, the lines and dots of dominoes. Children are always delighted with these little cakes.

Icing

1 cup confectioners' sugar	⅛ teaspoon salt
1½ tablespoons butter	1 teaspoon vanilla

Add confectioners' sugar to softened butter gradually. Blend these ingredients until they are creamy. You may substitute 1½ tablespoons of hot cream for the butter. Add salt and vanilla.

SOURCE: *The Ladies' Home Journal*, December 1899, p. 30.

Fruit Leaves

Cake recipe:

¾ cup sugar
4 egg yolks
1 teaspoon vanilla

¾ cup cake flour
¾ teaspoon any baking powder
¼ teaspoon salt

Sift sugar; beat egg yolks and add the sugar gradually. Beat until creamy and add vanilla. Sift the cake flour before measuring and resift with the baking powder. Add the flour gradually to the egg mixture. Beat the batter until it is smooth. Whip the egg whites until stiff, but not dry, and add salt. Fold the egg whites lightly into the batter until it is smooth. Line a 15-by-10-inch pan with heavy, greased, unglazed paper. Spread the batter in the pan and bake at 375 degrees F. for about twelve minutes.

After the cake is cool, cut pretty leaf shapes from it with a sharp pastry cutter; place on waxed paper and cover with a thin layer of green icing. Allow to dry. Serve in a circle or wreath on a pretty glass dish, and fill in the center with a mound of delicately whipped cream lightly sprinkled with finely chopped cherries.

SOURCE: *The Ladies' Home Journal*, December 1899, p. 30.

Mark Twain's Favorite Sweet Mince Cake
(This cake may be substituted for plum pudding).

1 cup butter
1 cup sugar
4 eggs
2 cups sifted
   all-purpose flour

½ teaspoon baking powder
1 teaspoon nutmeg
½ teaspoon salt
¼ cup brandy
¼ cup heavy cream

1 (9-ounce) package condensed
   mincemeat, crumbled
2 tablespoons flour

Cream butter and sugar. Add eggs, one at a time; beat well after each addition. Sift dry ingredients together. Combine brandy and cream. Add dry ingredients and brandy-cream mixture alternately to butter mixture, beginning and ending with the dry items. In a small bowl, combine crumbled mincemeat with two tablespoons of flour. Mix until mincemeat is well separated and well dredged with flour. Fold into batter. Spoon batter into a greased and wax-paper-lined 9-inch tube pan. Bake at 325 degrees F. for 1 hour and 20 minutes, until cake is golden brown and springs back when touched lightly with fingers. Cool in pan 10 minutes. Turn cake out and remove wax paper. Cool. Serve with coffee or tea. Tastes even better toasted.

SOURCE: Mark Twain Memorial, Hartford, Connecticut.

New Year's Calls and Receptions

In the 1800s, ladies preparing extensive entertainment for the New Year's holidays usually sent out, eight to ten days in advance, handsomely engraved cards of invitation for the New Year's reception. These invitations bore the name of the hostess, followed by the names of her grown daughters, if any. Enclosed in the same envelope were the visiting cards of ladies who had been invited to receive with the hostess.

If one of the ladies receiving with the hostess wished to invite her gentlemen friends to call on her, she sent them her own visiting card, with the number of the residence where she was to help receive, and the hour written, enclosing the card of her hostess.

The house where the reception was to be held would be arranged and ornamented with flowers and evergreens, and decorated, over-all, as attractively as possible.

A servant opened and shut the front door without waiting for the bell and had a silver tray ready to receive the cards of visitors.

After greeting her guests and wishing them a happy new year, the hostess offered refreshment, either handed from a side table by a servant, or offered from the dining room table, which was spread with choice articles of food. Since it was impossible for a guest to partake of substantial amounts of food at every house visited, the refreshments were kept light and tempting.

Many ladies of limited means and a quiet style of living did not send out invitations or make preparations for a reception, but held themselves in readiness throughout the day to receive calls in an informal way.

Since it was the custom, in large cities, for a gentleman to call on all the ladies he knew, it was permitted for those who had a wide circle of friends to leave cards showing that they had called in person, without actually visiting.

The length of the average call was fifteen minutes. Calls lasted from five minutes to half an hour.

The ladies wore handsome formal dress for these New Year's receptions, including gloves, which were left on.

Gentlemen callers were dressed in morning costume, as was the custom at all receptions.[17]

In the early 1900s, New Year's Day parties flourished in the southern United States; open house was kept from nine in the morning until midnight in at least one Atlanta household. From noon until six in the evening, hot food was served and in between times, guests would be offered eggnog

Winslow Homer's etching here shows young ladies at a New Year's Day reception awaiting the formal calls of the gentlemen they had invited.

and a cold plate. "One woman in Atlanta never issued any invitations to her New Year's receptions, but expected her friends at one time." In another part of the city, several families arranged to give their parties at the same hours, so that all the guests could go from one house to the other and make the rounds within two or three hours. Then, when the neighborhood parties were over, they could go to other parties.[18]

Margaret Mitchell, author of *Gone with the Wind*, described the decorations at these parties as lavish. Mistletoe was twined around cut-glass chandeliers. Stairways were draped with holly, vines, and other evergreens twining along the banisters. Eggnog bowls had holly wreaths around the sides, and fruit and flowers encircled the wreaths.[19]

St. Louis men, in the Victorian era, made New Year's calls in Prince Albert coats, light tan or gray trousers, light spats, silk hats, and white gloves. The gloves were considered necessities; the January 1 visitor would almost have preferred to omit his trousers rather than to leave behind his gloves, which were marks of gentility. Women's dresses were of gay-colored silks, covered with ruffles of French muslins trimmed with lace and ribbons.

The table held pyramids of spun sugar, with perhaps a boned turkey sliced and put back in its original shape; fruit cake; and a block of ice, hollowed out to hold Lynn Haven oysters, which were so huge that guests would have to hide behind a screen to eat them. In addition, there was terrapin, saddles of venison, hot beaten biscuits, chicken bouillon, ornamented ices, and glazed fruits.

A New Year's call showed appreciation for past favors and also wiped out any obligations.[20]

While Christmas was a family occasion, in New York City, as well as the rest of the country, New Year's Day was a time for open house. "Every woman that is 'anybody' stays at home in her best," author Lydia Maria Child noted in 1842. "By the hostess' side is a table covered with cakes, preserves, wines, oysters, hot coffee, etc., and as every gentleman is in honor bound to call on every lady of his acquaintance he does not intend to cut, the amount of eating and drinking done by some fashionable beaus must of course be very considerable. The number of calls is a matter of boasting among ladies, and there is considerable rivalry in the magnificence and variety of the eating tables."

Eggnog

Eggnog is a particularly Southern holiday specialty. It is usually traced back to syllabub, but the English drink contained no eggs; and eggnog never became popular in New York, where syllabub was a favorite New Year's Day drink. It seems more likely that eggnog is related to German egg punch, made with milk and wine, and still popular in Germany today.

Recipes for eggnog are many and varied, from the very rich Kentucky bourbon version to those requiring a variety of liquors. When making a quantity of eggnog to serve over a period of time, it is more satisfactory to divide the egg whites and use only as needed, beating them up at the time of serving. The recipe that follows is excellent.

Eggnog

6 eggs, separated	2 teaspoons vanilla
½ cup sugar (to taste)	3 cups heavy cream
1½ cups bourbon	1 pint milk
½ cup rum	3 tablespoons sugar
½ cup brandy or Cointreau	
Nutmeg	

Beat egg yolks well, adding sugar gradually. While still beating, add liquor gradually. Add vanilla and put mixture into refrigerator to chill at least one hour. Then add cream and milk from time to time, preferably over a period of twenty-four hours. Stir well with each addition.

When ready to serve, beat egg whites (or as many as needed for first serving) until stiff. Fold half into mixture. Add 3 tablespoons sugar to remaining portion and swirl on top of individual cups. Sprinkle with nutmeg.

Eggnog can be frozen satisfactorily, but will not freeze hard because of the large quantity of alcohol it contains.

This recipe serves approximately twenty-five.

SOURCE: Ruth Cole Kainen, *America's Christmas Heritage*, (New York: Funk and Wagnall's, 1969), p. 116. Reprinted by permission of Harper and Row, Publisher.

New Year's Day Bill of Fare

Bouillon	Chocolate with
Jellied Chicken	Whipped Cream
Boned Turkey	Ices
Pressed Tongue	New Year's Cake
Pickled Oysters	Fruit Cake
Lobster Mayonnaise	Small Cakes
Crackers and Wafers	Lemonade, Coffee
Fancy Pickles	Eggnog
Calf's-Foot Jelly	
(with Charlotte Russe)	

SOURCE: *The Ladies' Home Journal*, January 1889, p. 14.

Jellied Chicken

1 4-pound chicken	Sliced pimento-stuffed olives
1 carrot	Sliced hard-boiled eggs
1 onion	1 teaspoon gelatine
1 stalk celery	¼ cup cold chicken stock
Salt and pepper	1 cup hot chicken stock

Stew a four-pound chicken in enough water to cover. Add onion, carrot, and celery to enrich stock. Simmer until very tender. Drain the chicken and reserve the stock.

Cut the chicken from the bones; add salt and pepper. Oil a mold and garnish with slices of pimento-stuffed olives and slices of hard-boiled eggs.

Soak one teaspoon of gelatine (unflavored) in ¼-cup cold stock until it is dissolved; then add the cup of boiling stock. Chill until almost set, then stir in the chicken and spoon it into the mold. Chill.

Pressed Tongue

Wash two large beef tongues. Put them into a kettle and cover with cold water. Place over a moderate fire and simmer gently until the meat falls to pieces; add a teaspoonful of salt. Chop the meat. Boil the liquor down until reduced to a quart; strain it, season, and mix it with the tongue. Pour the mixture into a mold and refrigerate, with a weight placed on top. When hard and cold, turn out and slice thin.

Pickled Oysters

Boil five dozen oysters five minutes; drain. Take a pint of vinegar and pour in the oyster liquor, set on the stove, season with ¼ teaspoon each of mace, cloves, allspice, black pepper, and cayenne pepper. As soon as the liquid is boiling hot, pour it over the oysters and set them away in the refrigerator to cool.

Lobster Mayonnaise

Boil four lobsters. When they have cooled, take out the meat, cut small, and set on ice. Mix the chopped lobster with mayonnaise and garnish with sliced hard-boiled eggs.

Calf's-Foot Jelly

Lemon gelatine, made according to the directions on the box, with a small jar of grape jelly added to it makes a good substitute for calf's-foot jelly.

Charlotte Russe

1 cup milk	¼ teaspoon salt
1 envelope unflavored gelatine	Grated rind of 1 lemon
2 tablespoons cold water	¼ cup lemon juice
4 egg yolks	6 ladyfingers, split
½ cup sugar	1 cup heavy cream

Scald milk. Sprinkle gelatine over cold water to soften. Mix together egg yolks, sugar, and salt. Pour hot milk, a little at a time, over the yolk mixture, beating hard all the time. Cook over low heat, stirring constantly, until mixture is smooth and slightly thickened. Remove from heat, add gelatine, and stir until dissolved. Stir in lemon rind and juice, then refrigerate until cold, but not set. Line a one-quart mold or bowl with ladyfingers, placing some on the bottom and the remainder upright around the sides. Some of the ladyfingers may have to be cut to make them fit. Beat heavy cream until it holds its shape; fold into gelatin mixture gently and pour into mold. Chill two to three hours or until firm. To serve, unmold on a crystal or silver platter or cake-stand. Serves six.

Source: *The American Heritage Cookbook* (New York: American Heritage Publishing Company, Inc., 1964), p. 570.

Black Fruitcake

¼ pound candied citron	¼ pound shelled walnuts or pecans
⅛ pound candied lemon peel	2 cups sifted all-purpose flour
⅛ pound candied orange peel	½ teaspoon mace
½ pound candied cherries	½ teaspoon cinnamon
1 pound candied pineapple	½ teaspoon baking soda
1 pound golden raisins	½ cup (1 stick) butter
½ pound seeded raisins	1 cup sugar
¼ pound currants	1 cup brown sugar, packed
½ cup dark rum, cognac, sherry or Madeira	5 eggs
	1 tablespoon milk
¼ pound blanched shelled almonds	1 teaspoon almond extract

This recipe is of English origin and is known variously as Dark Fruitcake, English Fruitcake, Black Fruitcake, and Merry Christmas cake.

The fruits and nuts should be prepared the day before, as follows: sliver the citron, lemon, and orange peel into very thin strips; cut the cherries in half and the pineapple in thin wedges. Set aside. Pick over the raisins and currants to eliminate stray stems or seeds; add rum, cognac, sherry, or Madeira, and soak overnight. Chop the almonds and the walnuts or pecans coarsely. Set them aside, too. The following day, prepare the pan. Grease a 10-inch tube pan, four 1-pound coffee cans, or two bread pans measuring 9 by 5 by 3 inches. Line with brown paper.

To make the cake: Mix a half-cup of the sifted flour with all the fruits and nuts in a large bowl. Sift remaining flour with spices and baking soda. Cream butter until soft, then work in granulated sugar and brown sugar, a little at a time, until mixture is smooth. Stir in the eggs, milk, almond extract, and, finally, the flour mixture. Mix thoroughly. Pour over the fruit and nuts and work together, with your hands, until batter is very well mixed. Lift the batter into the pan or pans and press it down firmly to make

126

a compact cake when cooked. Bake in a preheated 275-degree oven. A tube pan that uses all the batter will take 3¼ hours; the bread pans, which will each hold half the batter, 2¼ hours; the coffee cans, which each hold ¼ of the batter, 2 hours. Remove cakes from oven; let stand half an hour, then turn out onto cake racks. Peel off the brown paper very carefully. The four small, round cakes make attractive Christmas presents.

To age fruitcakes: Allow at least four weeks. Wrap each cake in several layers of cheesecloth well soaked in rum, cognac, sherry, or Madeira. Place in an airtight container, such as a large crock or kettle, and cover tightly. If cheesecloth dries out, moisten it with a little of the wine or spirits. Do not overdo it. The cakes should be firm, not soft, at the end of the aging period. . . . To decorate, make a garland of candied cherries, slivered angelica, and blanched whole almonds around the edge of the cake.

SOURCE: *The American Heritage Cookbook* (New York: American Heritage Publishing Company, Inc., 1964), p. 603.

New Year's Day Cake

1½ cups sugar	1 cup milk
1 cup butter	4 egg whites
4 egg yolks	¼ teaspoon salt
1½ teaspoons vanilla	1 cup coconut
2⅔ cups cake flour	1½ cups slivered almonds
2 teaspoons baking powder	(blanched)
½ teaspoon salt	1 cup raisins
½ teaspoon cloves	1 tablespoon cinnamon

Mix butter and sugar until creamy. Beat in egg yolks, one at a time. Add vanilla. Sift and add flour, baking powder, and salt in three parts alternately with the milk. Beat until smooth after each addition.

Whip the egg whites until stiff, but not dry, with ¼ teaspoon salt. Fold lightly into the batter.

Divide the batter into two equal parts. To the first, add the coconut and one cup of almonds. To the second half, add the raisins, first shaking them with flour so they will not stick to the bottom of the pan; then add the other ½ cup of nuts. Add cinnamon, nutmeg, and cloves.

Bake in two 9-inch oiled cake pans at 350 degrees F. for 45 minutes.

Frost with butter frosting.

Little Christmas

Parties celebrating Twelfth Night held on January 5 brought to a close the Christmas season. It was customary to serve a special cake on that day, along with other things mentioned previously that could be served at a Christmas party.

Along with the usual Christmas entertainment, the cake furnished a game that could be played two ways. A bean could be hidden in the cake, and the person finding it would be proclaimed king and choose a queen; or a pea could be placed in the cake, and the lady finding it would be crowned queen.

Twelfth Night: Choosing King and Queen

Was-haile!
Your places, lads and lasses, take
To find your fortune in the cake.
Was-haile!
Jock gets the bean,
And chooses Kate for queen,
Drink-haile!
Now foot it in the reel,
Each frolic heel;
Ye maskers, that a-mumming go,
Stay yet, and point the toe;
"Bounce, buckram, velvets dear,
For Christmas comes but once a year!"
Was-haile! Drink-haile! Noel!
Goodnight! Sleep well!
God keep us all, Immanuel![21]

Epiphany Cake

2 eggs	1½ cups sifted flour
1 cup sugar	½ teaspoon baking soda
1 teaspoon vanilla	½ teaspoon salt
1 cup sour cream	1 teaspoon baking powder

Beat eggs and sugar. Add flavorings to sour cream, then add alternately to the egg mixture with the sifted dry ingredients. Bake in greased 9-inch-square pan at 350 degrees F. for 35 to 40 minutes.

Wrap the following items in foil and insert into the batter before baking. The finder of each item is supposed to reflect the qualities or capabilities the token is whimsically said to represent.

Button *(faithfulness)*	Ring *(faithfulness)*
Dime *(wealth)*	Thimble *(patience)*
Bean *(king)*	Pea *(queen)*
Heart *(devotion)*	Clove *(fool, jester)*

Appendix A
Patterns

Most drawings in this section are the correct size to use as patterns for projects explained in the text. Where size is not exact, because of limited space, measurements for exact size are given.

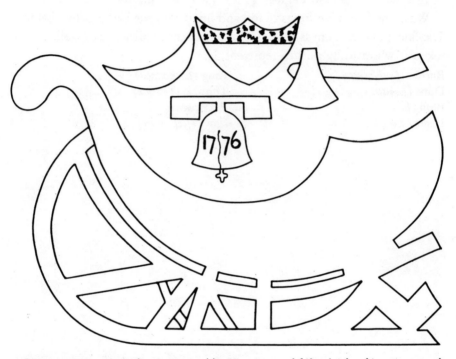

Paper tree ornaments (see directions, page 44). Victorians used foil or bright, shiny paper to make ornaments like these, in the shape of familiar objects.

Add four wheels, fold sides and back upward, and this paper tree decoration is a haywagon. Sides folded downward make runners and turn it into a sledge. Directions on page 44.

131

Patterns for the eggshell pitcher (directions on page 59).
Follow drawings to make spout, handle, and bottom rim.

TOP & BOTTOM

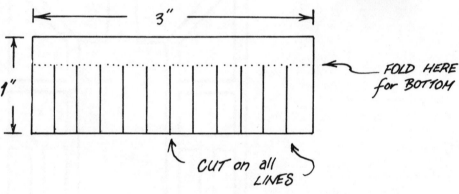

← 3″ →

FOLD HERE
for BOTTOM

1″

CUT on all
LINES

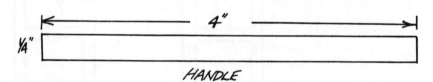

← 4″ →

¼″

HANDLE

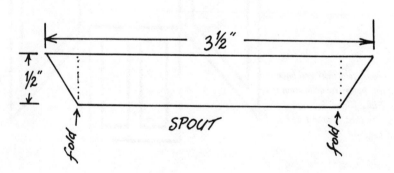

← 3½″ →

½″

fold →

SPOUT

fold →

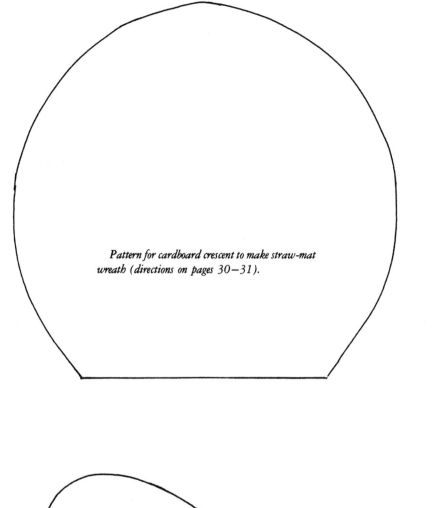

Pattern for cardboard crescent to make straw-mat wreath (directions on pages 30–31).

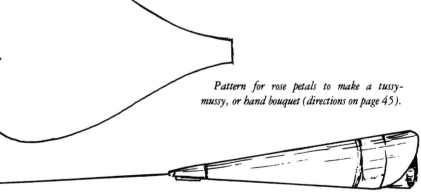

Pattern for rose petals to make a tussy-mussy, or hand bouquet (directions on page 45).

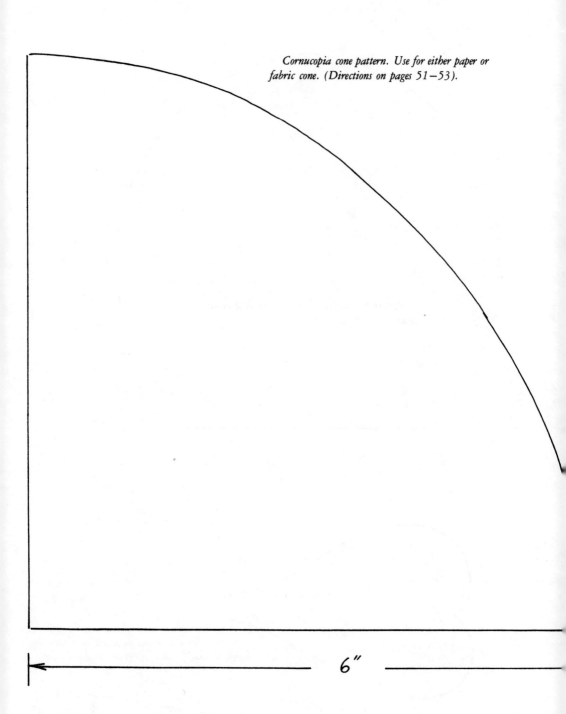

Cornucopia cone pattern. Use for either paper or fabric cone. (Directions on pages 51–53).

6"

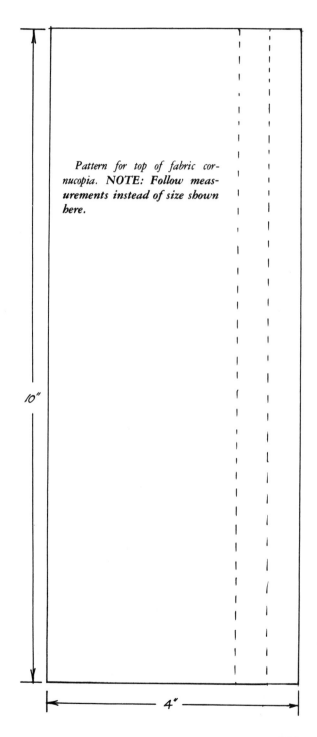

Pattern for top of fabric cornucopia. NOTE: Follow measurements instead of size shown here.

10"

4"

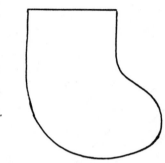

Boot Pattern.

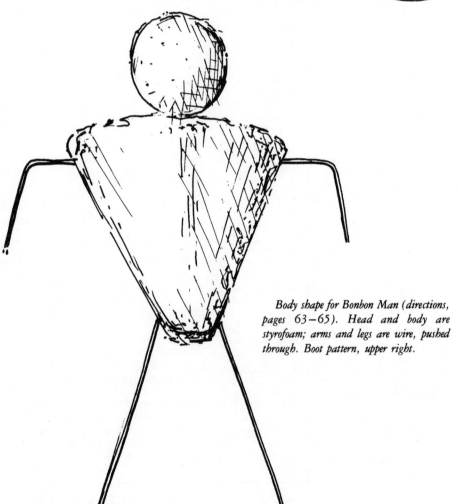

Body shape for Bonbon Man (directions, pages 63–65). Head and body are styrofoam; arms and legs are wire, pushed through. Boot pattern, upper right.

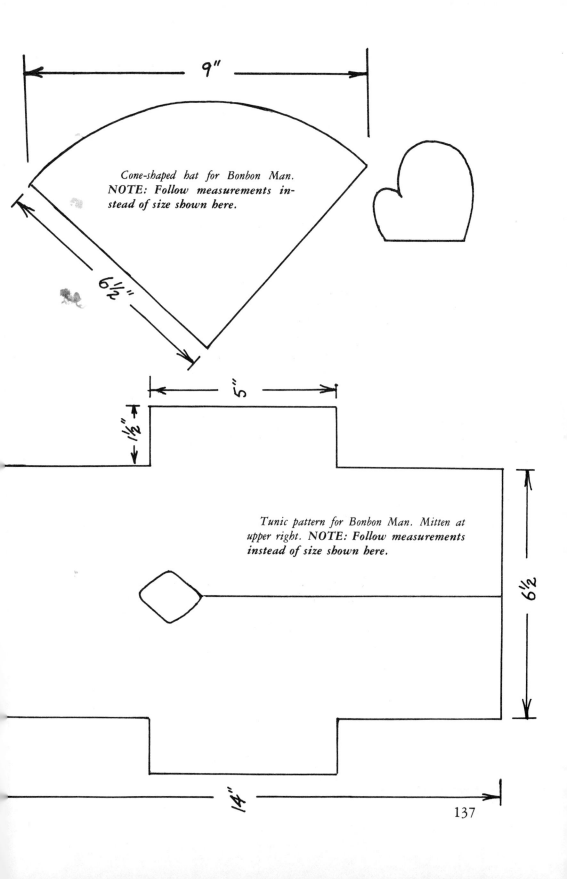

9"

Cone-shaped hat for Bonbon Man. **NOTE: Follow measurements instead of size shown here.**

6½"

5"

1½"

Tunic pattern for Bonbon Man. Mitten at upper right. **NOTE: Follow measurements instead of size shown here.**

6½

14"

137

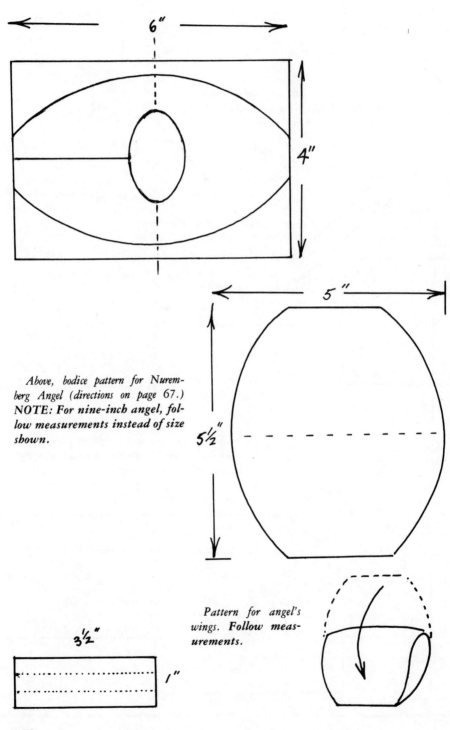

Above, bodice pattern for Nuremberg Angel (directions on page 67.) **NOTE: For nine-inch angel, follow measurements instead of size shown.**

Pattern for angel's wings. Follow measurements.

138

*Patterns for Nuremberg Angel's accordian-pleated underskirt (top) and overskirt (bottom). (Directions on page 67. **Follow measurements instead of size shown.**)*

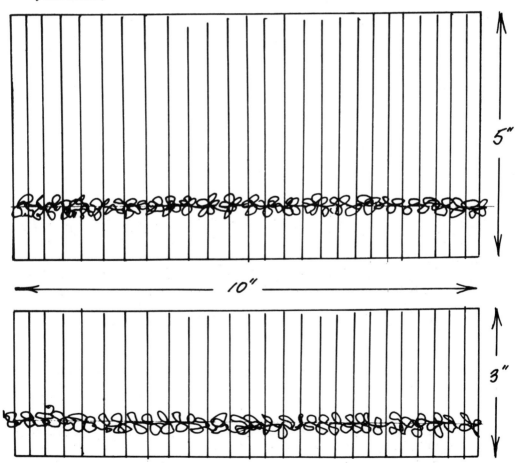

Appendix B
Sources for Supplies

Reproductions of Victorian paper seals, Christmas cards, clip-on metal candle-holders, small toys, miniatures:

    Federal Smallwares Corporation   Catalogue, $1.00
    85 Fifth Avenue (at 16th Street)
    New York, New York 10003

Reproductions of Victorian paper dolls, gift-wrappings, patterns for miniature rooms:

    Hobby House Press, Inc.   Catalogue, free
    900 Frederick Street
    Cumberland, Maryland 21502

Christmas seals, Victorian paper dolls, booklets on pressing and drying flowers:

    Sunny O'Neil   Price list, stamped self-
    7106 River Road   addressed envelope
    Bethesda, Maryland 20817

Craft supplies: Floral foam, wire, ribbon, straw wreaths:

    Boycan's   Catalogue, $1.00
    P.O. Box 897
    Sharon, Pennsylvania 16146

Needlework and Crafts:

    Lee Ward's   Catalogue, free
    1200 St. Charles Road
    Elgin, Illinois 60120

Fragrances: Castile soap, oils, or powders

    Caswell-Massey Company, Ltd.   Catalogue, $1.00
    320 West 13th Street
    New York, New York 10014

    C'est l'Alchimiste   Price list, stamped self-
    5300 Wisconsin Avenue, N.W.   addressed envelope
    Washington, D.C. 20015

Dried flowers and herbs:

    Well-Sweep Herb Farm   Catalogue, $ .75
    317 Mt. Bethel Road
    Port Murray, New Jersey 07865

Stillridge Herb Farm   Catalogue, $ .50
10370 Route 99
Woodstock, Maryland 21163

Handcrafted cookie cutters:
    The Old Salem Store   Price list, stamped, self-
    500 S. Main Street   addressed envelope
    Winston-Salem, North Carolina 27101

Pomander ball supplies, herbs, fresh and dried:
    Caprilands Herb Farm   Price list, large, stamped, self-
    Silver Street   addressed envelope
    Coventry, Connecticut 06238

Notes

Notes, Chapter I

1. *The Ladies' Home Journal*, December 1890, p. 10.
2. *The Ladies' Home Journal*, October 1890, p. 8.
3. Mark Twain Memorial, Hartford, Connecticut.
4. *The Ladies' Home Journal*, December 1895, p. 29.
5. Harnett T. Kane, *The Southern Christmas Book* (New York: David McKay, Inc., 1958), p. 167.
6. Mark Twain Memorial, Hartford, Connecticut.
7. Brochure, "Oatlands" (Washington, D.C.: National Trust for Historic Preservation, n.d.).
8. Harnett T. Kane, *The Southern Christmas Book*, p. 206.
9. *Saint Nicholas*, December 1876, p. 156.
10. *The Ladies' Home Journal*, March 1900, p. 22.
11. *American Agriculturist,* December 1895, p. 575.
12. Adelia Beard, *Girl's Handy Book* (New York: Scribner's Pub. Co., 1898), p. 319.
13. *The Ladies' Home Journal*, December 1892, p. 20.
14. *The Ladies' Home Journal*, December 1897, p. 10.

Notes, Chapter II

1. *The Ladies' Home Journal*, December 1890, p. 9.
2. *American Agriculturist*, December 1878, p. 426.
3. *American Agriculturist*, December 1878, p. 425; December 1884, p. 549.
4. *Vick's Floral Guide*, January 1879, p. 47.
5. *The Ladies' Home Journal*, December 1889, p. 19.
6. *The Ladies' Home Journal*, December 1892, p. 24.
7. *The Ladies' Home Journal*, December 1892, p. 24.
8. *Vick's Floral Guide*, January 1879, p. 48.
9. *American Agriculturist*, December 1889, p. 640.
10. *The Ladies' Home Journal*, December 1889, p. 19; December 1895, p. 28; December 1895, p. 19.
11. *The Ladies' Home Journal*, December 1895, p. 28.
12. *The Ladies' Home Journal*, December 1889, p. 19.
13. *Harper's Young People*, December 7, 1880, p. 86.
14. *The Ladies' Home Journal*, December 1893, p. 6.

Notes, Chapter III

1. Charles Dickens, *A Christmas Tree* (Lancaster, Pa.: J. P. McCaskey, 1913), p. 3.
2. *Godey's Lady's Book*, December 1860, p. 481.
3. *Godey's Lady's Book,* December 1860, p. 481.
4. *Peterson's Magazine*, December 1880.
5. Phillip V. Snyder, *The Christmas Tree Book* (New York: Viking Press, 1976), p. 154.
6. *The Ladies' Home Journal*, December 1890, p. 9.
7. *Godey's Lady's Book*, December 1880, p. 555.
8. *Godey's Lady's Book*, December 1880, p. 555.
9. Snyder, *The Christmas Tree Book*, p. 142.
10. Caroline L. Smith, *American Home Book of Indoor Games.* (Boston: Lee and Shepard, Publishers, 1874).
11. *The Ladies' Home Journal*, December, 1892, p. 27.
12. Adelia Beard and Lina Beard, *What a Girl can Make and Do* (New York: Scribner's Publishing Co., 1902), p. 244.

Notes, Chapter IV

1. *The Ladies' Home Journal*, November 1892, p. 31.
2. *Graham's Magazine*, December 1857, p. 88.
3. *The Ladies' Home Journal*, December 1892, p. 24.
4. Kane, *The Southern Christmas Book*, p. 72.
5. Brochure, "Oatlands" (Washington, D.C.: The National Trust for Historic Preservation, n.d.).

Notes, Chapter V

1. *The Ladies' Home Journal*, November 1897, p. 18.
2. *The Ladies' Home Journal*, November 1897, p. 18.
3. *The Ladies' Home Journal*, November 1897, p. 18.
4. *Farm Journal*, October 1882.
5. *American Agriculturist*, December 1889, p. 645.
6. *American Agriculturist*, December 1889, p. 645.
7. *American Agriculturist*, December 1889, p. 645.
8. *American Agriculturist*, December 1889, p. 645.
9. *American Agriculturist*, December 1897, p. 508.
10. *American Agriculturist*, December 1862, p. 373.
11. Mary E. Blain, *Games for All Occasions* (New York: Barse and Co., 1909), pp. 140–141.
12. *The Ladies' Home Journal*, December 1897, p. 31.
13. *The Ladies' Home Journal*, December 1892, p. 27.
14. *The Ladies' Home Journal*, December 1891, p. 45.
15. *The Ladies' Home Journal*, May 1889, p. 11.
16. *The Ladies' Home Journal*, December 1890, p. 29.
17. *The Ladies' Home Journal*, January 1889, p. 4.
18. Kane, *The Southern Christmas Book*, p. 123.
19. Kane, *The Southern Christmas Book*, p. 167.
20. Kane, *The Southern Christmas Book*, p. 180.
21. *Harper's New Monthly Magazine*, December 1880, pp. 6–7.

Bibliography

Victorian Periodicals Consulted

American Agriculturist	*Graham's Magazine*	*St. Nicholas Magazine*
Farm Journal	*Harper's New Monthly Magazine*	*Peterson's Magazine*
Godey's Lady's Book	*Harper's Young People*	*Vick's Floral Guide*

Books

American Heritage Publishing Company, Inc. *American Heritage Cookbook*. New York: American Heritage Publishing Company, Inc., 1964.

Andrews, Mrs. Lewis R., and Mrs. J. Reancy Kelly. *Maryland's Way*. Baltimore: The Hammond-Harwood House Association, 1963.

Beard, Adelia. *Girl's Handy Book*. New York: Scribner's Publishing Company, 1898.

Beard, Adelia, and Lina Beard. *Things Worth Doing and How to Do Them*. New York: Scribner's Publishing Company, 1906.

Beard, Adelia, and Lina Beard. *What a Girl Can Make and Do*. New York: Scribner's Publishing Company, 1902.

Blain, Mary E. *Games for All Occasions*. New York: Barse and Company, 1909.

Butterick Publishing Company, Inc. *Needle and Brush*, Metropolitan Art Series. New York: Butterick Publishing Company, Inc., 1889.

Colonial Williamsburg Foundation. *Christmas Decorations from Williamsburg's Folk Art Collection*. Williamsburg, Va.: Colonial Williamsburg Foundation, Publishers, 1976. Distributed by Holt, Rinehart and Winston.

Dick and Fitzgerald. *Fireside Games*. New York: Dick and Fitzgerald, 1859.

Farmer, Fannie Merritt. *The Boston Cooking School Cookbook*. Boston: Little, Brown Publishing Company, 1947.

Kainen, Ruth Cole. *America's Christmas Heritage*. New York: Funk and Wagnall's, 1969.

Kane, Harnett T. *The Southern Christmas Book*. New York: David McKay, Inc., 1958.

Pasley, Virginia. *The Holiday Candy Book*. Boston: Little, Brown and Company, 1952, in association with the Atlantic Monthly Press.

Smith, Caroline L. *American Home Book of Indoor Games*. Boston: Lee and Shepard Publishing Company, 1874.

Snyder, Phillip V. *The Christmas Tree Book*. New York: The Viking Press, 1976.

Williams, H. T. *The Ladies' Floral Cabinet*. New York: H. T. Williams, 1884.

Zenker, John, and Hazel Zenker. *Cookie Cookery*. New York: M. Evans and Company, Inc., 1969.

Picture Credits

Author and publisher make grateful acknowledgment to the individuals and organizations listed below, for permission to reproduce pictorial materials from their collections:

Color Plates: Columbia Historical Society, Washington, D.C., and Perry Gerard Fisher, executive director, for views of the Christian Heurich Mansion with design and decoration by Sunny O'Neil, photographs by Linda Bartlett: *front cover*, Plates 1, 10, and 11. The Smithsonian Institution, for views of the Trees of Christmas Exhibit mounted by the Smithsonian Institution Office of Horticulture: Plates 2, 3, 4, 5, 6, 8, and 9, photographed by Rhoda Baer; and Plate 7, photographed by Darwin K. Davidson.

Black and white: Abby Aldrich Rockefeller Folk Art Center, Williamsburg, Va., pages 47, 54. Earl Gregg Swem Library, College of William and Mary, pages 5, 6, 10, 13, 14, 27 *middle*, 32, 84, 90, and 109, from files of the *Ladies' Home Journal*, 1840–1900; *facing page* 1, pages 3, 8, 9 *top*, 22, 27 *bottom*, 30, 31, 98, 122, and 133 *top*, from files of *Harper's Young People*, *Harper's Weekly*, and *Harper's Bazaar*, 1800–1900. Library of Congress, Rare Books and Special Collections Division, pages 9 *bottom*, 24 *right*, 49, 57, 61, and 101; from *Godey's Lady's Book* files, 1860–1880s, *title page*, pages 38, 44, 46, 63, 64, 65 *top*, 69, 70, 130, 131, 136, and 137. Morris Library, University of Delaware, pages 20, 21, 23, 24 *left*, 27 *top*, and 28, from files of *Vick's Floral Guide*, 1860–1890. National Agricultural Library, Educational Research Division, U.S. Department of Agriculture, pages 11, 26, 33, 34, 35, 87, 106, from files of *American Agriculturist*, 1860–1890. National Trust for Historic Preservation, page 12, from Oatlands Mansion brochure. Dennis O'Neil, pages 8, 9, 10, 11, 12, 13, 14, 25, 26, 31, 33, 34, 35, 45, 48, 49, 50, 51, 52, 57, 58, 59, 64, 65, 66, 67, 68, 70, 87, 101, and enlargements on pages 132–139, adapted from notes and/or drawings in sources noted in text. Phillip V. Snyder, pages 48, 50, 65 *bottom*, 66, 67, 68, 138, and 139.